From the Western Door to the Lower West Side

Also by Eric Gansworth

Novels
*Indian Summers**
*Smoke Dancing**
*Mending Skins**

Poetry Collections
*Nickel Eclipse: Iroquois Moon**
*A Half-Life of Cardio-Pulmonary Function**

Creative Non-Fiction, Poems
*Breathing the Monster Alive**

Drama
*Re-Creation Story**

Editor:
Sovereign Bones: New Native American Writing, Volume II

*includes visual art by the author

Also by Milton Rogovin

Milton Rogovin: The Forgotten Ones by Cheryl A. Brutvan, Robert J. Doherty and Fred Licht
Milton Rogovin: The Forgotten Ones by Dave Isay
Windows That Open Inward - Poetry by Pablo Neruda, Photographs by Milton Rogovin
Triptychs: Buffalo's Lower West Side Revisited
Portraits in Steel: Milton Rogovin and Mike Frisch
Milton Rogovin: The Bonds Between Us
With Eyes and Soul: Images of Cuba - Photographs by Milton Rogovin, Poetry by Nancy Morejon
Milton Rogvin: The Mining Photographs
Milton Rogovin: The Making of a Social Documentary Photographer, with text by Melanie Herzog
Nada Queda Atrás - Photographs by Milton Rogovin, Poetry by Carlos Trujillo
The Lens & The Pen: Photographs and Poems by Milton Rogovin

From the Western Door to the Lower West Side

Photographs by Milton Rogovin

Poems by Eric Gansworth

White Pine Press / Buffalo, New York

Copyright ©2010 by White Pine Press
Text Copyright ©2010 by Eric Gansworth
Photographs copyright ©1952–2002 by Milton Rogovin

All rights reserved. This work, or portions thereof, may not be reproduced
in any form without the written permission of the publisher.

Publication of this book was made possible, in part,
with public funds from the New York State Council on the Arts, a State Agency.

ACKNOWLEDGMENTS: As in all past projects, thank you first and foremost to Larry Plant, who believed, even earlier than I did, that I was the right person for this book, sparking thought and conversation in those beginning struggles. Thanks, of course, to Milton and Mark Rogovin, Ellen Rogovin Hart, Paula Rogovin, and Michelle Melin-Rogovin for their invitation to this project and then, their later patience in the year it took me to find a way to deal with the work's demands. Thanks to Dennis Maloney, long-time friend and passionate supporter of poetry in Western New York and the world. Thanks to Catherine Linder Spencer, friend and photographic artist, who introduced me to the Rogovin family, and who, over the years, shared so many stories of her friend Milton that I felt like I knew him even before we had met.

Thank you to Bob Baxter, who read a draft of this book, in the middle of many other projects of his own. Thanks to Bruce Adams, for his initial enthusiasm for this project, in the pages of *Buffalo Spree*, and for his sincerity and generosity, even in very trying moments. "Big Frankie" lives on. Thanks to Kate Koperski of the Castellani Art Museum, for showing the first pieces from this collaboration. *Nyah-wheh* to my family, always, for their good humor when they discover themselves on my pages.

Thank you to Canisius College for its support of my work, specifically President Reverend Vincent M. Cooke, S.J.; Vice President for Academic Affairs Scott A. Chadwick; Dean of Arts and Sciences Paula M. McNutt and later, Leonid A. Khinkis; and the Joseph S. Lowery Estate for Funding Faculty Fellowship in Creative Writing.

Special thanks to the Center for Creative Photography, University of Arizona, Tucson, the Rogovin Collection, LLC, and to Gene Witkowski for providing scans of the photographs used in this book. Thanks also to Alexis Ellers and Rachel Swenie.

The Rogovin family expresses its deep appreciation to Eric Gansworth for his powerful poetry which brings such insight to Milton's photographs.

With appreciation to Anne Rogovin (1918–2003) for all she did to raise a family, teach, write, and travel the world with Milton. She was involved with all aspects of Milton's photography.

First Edition
ISBN: 978-1-935210-10-8
Printed and bound in the United States of America.
Library of Congress Control Number: 2009932982
WHITE PINE PRESS   P.O. Box 236   BUFFALO, NEW YORK 14201

www.whitepine.org

for the Bumblebee
at a quarter century,
navigating those two rows
with grace and patience,

and for the people
who inhabit these pages,
wherever they find themselves,
with respect and honor.

Contents

Artery / 11

Two Rows / 12

What the Photographer Said / 17

Dusk to Dusk / 22

What the Photographer Saw / 29

Harvest and Germination / 38

Her Creations / 40

The Grandmothers / 46

Baby Picture / 54

Family Connection, Once Removed / 59

Three More Sisters / 60

Beads / 63

Books / 67

Beds / 69

While Hendrix Played a Solo: "Burning of the Midnight Lamp" / 72

While Hendrix Played a Solo: "Gypsy Eyes" / 75

While Hendrix Played a Solo: "Purple Haze" / 77

West Side Social / 80

Tiny Chief / 89

Door to Door / 98

About Milton Rogovin / 112

About Eric Gansworth / 113

From the Western Door to the Lower West Side

Artery

The garage's dark interior
lined high with shelves
of grease-filmed bottles
protects this man's lifeline,
a fusion of chemicals and dreams
coursing through the fuel lines,
keeping his carburetor clean.

The car and owner know the road
and the way miles add up
despite a desire to keep
those numbers from climbing.

Though he trusts the photographer
enough to stand before
his keys to both homes,
he keeps the plate numbers
protected behind his crossed legs,
because some people still believe
"the Only Good Indian
is a Dead Indian,"
and he knows he is too old
to walk from
the Lower West Side
to the Western Door,
and the only way
to ride that forty mile lifeline connecting
the two halves of his divided heart
is his faithful Buick
and those combustion dreams
he protects behind crossed arms.

Two Rows

The Two Row Wampum Belt is, in its design, simplicity itself. It is the first treaty belt between the Haudenosaunee and Europeans who arrived on this continent—in this case the Dutch who were migrating into Haudenosaunee territory, what is now commonly referred to as Upstate New York. The belt defined the relationship between these two cultural entities as equals, siblings, not father and son, the way Europeans were attracted to defining the relationship. The European colonists had desired to treat the Haudenosaunee as childlike, less sophisticated because the culture had a different aesthetic, one the Dutch were quick to interpret as less advanced. The belt is intended to clarify and correct that misconception. It is made up of two identical rows of purple wampum beads on a background of three rows of white wampum beads, in equal ratio. The belt's iconic lines are meant to represent two canoes, traveling side by side, as equals, neither interfering in the other's business as they make their way down the river of history and future, each respectfully acknowledging the presence of the other. Of course, the history of this continent informs us that things are often much more complicated than the best intentions of our ancestors. This is not to say there isn't immense truth to be had in understanding these orderly rows of beads. I suspect that we, members of the Haudenosaunee, are familiar with the resonance of this imagery broadly, as a culture, and on more personal, intimate levels, almost as consistently. That universal movement between the cultural and the personal is the eternal bridge that art creates for us.

John C. Mohawk's monograph, *Iroquois Creation Story: John Arthur Gibson and J.N.B. Hewitt's "Myth of the Earth Grasper,"* an introductory contemporizing text of the Haudenosaunee Creation Story, offered a concise insight into the way we, Haudenosaunee people, respond to circumstances beyond our control. I saw much of my own personal history in his observations. I'm the first to admit that I've had a strange life, one filled with enough bizarre coincidence that I tend to forgive stories in which the unlikely and improbable happen because the person telling the story needs them to happen, rather than out of any sense of the way the world usually works. Perhaps odd exchanges happen among many people, but they grow tired or disenchanted with reality and then disregard the existence of other possibilities. Some people have suggested directly to me that I am enormously gullible and that I have believed the stories of others I should have known better than to trust.

Among his assertions, John suggested that our Creation Story has a spiritual pragmatism at its core—that we, as a culture, respond to whatever comes our way, understanding we will encounter difficult times in our lives, but that we are generally thankful for the good times we have between those difficulties. He suggested that we thoughtfully examine the events of our lives as they arrive, and evaluate their potential effect, as clearly as we can. I am fortunate to have been born into a culture where that lens is a driving philosophy. It has served me well, if to the consternation of others.

At different times in my life, I have appeared elated with things deemed unworthy of such zeal by others. On other occasions, I have apparently responded to good news or opportunities suspiciously. Most times, I do not make overt responses to much of any news, because often enough, my heightened response has opposed the messenger's expectations. It has been safer to take the information in and consider it seriously. I would be terrible as a game show contestant. There isn't much in my life that has caused me to jump up and down, animated and out of control, though some would suggest I have had plenty of reasons to do just that, in good terms and bad.

When I first looked at the images from Milton Rogovin's Native American Series formally, it was at the invitation of Milton and his son Mark. The context was a potential collaboration on the occasion of these images' first mounting as an explicitly identified series. I had seen some of the photographs before, in a show at the Burchfield Penney Art Center, with a couple hundred pieces by contemporary indigenous artists, and early twentieth century photographs of American Indians. That show was curated in an "issues of representation" orientation. So for the first time I saw this series in isolation, it was laid out as a stack of reproductions on Milton's kitchen table. While Milton flipped through my first collection of poems—I guess to see if I were indeed the right person for this invitation—Mark and I looked at the images, one by one. I recognized some faces. Other images were familiar in tone. The cast-iron manual water-pump in one photo seemed to be the model identical to the one I had grown up using, its handle warm on summer mornings and almost unendurably cold in January and February. Wooden planks sunk in mud leading up to an old house's front door, a woodpile, an outhouse—these were all sights that had a permanent residence in my memory.

Though I had previously had only minimal exposure to this body of work, I understood the great dangers inherent in such a project. There was first, naturally, the long and complicated history of American Indians and others who have portrayed us in photographic media, manipulated to the photographer's desires, rather than the subject's. While not uncommon (Who has not been instructed by a photographer to move this way or that?), it is still fraught with complications.

That difficulty was largely thanks to Edward Curtis's aesthetic campaign to insist that the American Indians he photographed were part of a vanishing culture. I still have people commenting to me about his lovely and "powerful" (always "powerful") portraits of American Indians, completely oblivious to the fact that Curtis manipulated and posed his subjects to make them appear as if they belong to cultures which were dying. The long debate concerning cross-cultural relationships between artist and subject also has been particularly lively in the last couple of decades.

I am keenly aware of this debate. As a writer who works in fiction as much as poetry, I often insert my imagination into the lives of others—the barely seen gesture, the overheard whisper, the violated secret—these are all seeds of potentially wondrous stories. I understood though, looking at the people and places in these photos, even some I knew, that fabricated and manipulated versions of their lives were not the compositional process that was called for. As we looked at the images, Mark must have sensed my reticence. At one point, he said exasperated, point blank: "Do any of these photos interest you? And if not, is there another poet you think might be interested in working with them?"

They were fair questions. I explained that yes, they did interest me, and that often, people are annoyed at my lack of affect. I did know of other poets, of course, some who have worked in dialogue with the work of others. I would give the idea some serious consideration and if it were not for me, I would happily pass along contact information of those other poets. Milton and Mark gave me a complete set of photocopy reproductions, and a copy of Milton's recently published biography, a project with which I had been long familiar. A friend of mine, Catherine Linder Spencer, had spent many years, working intimately with Milton, as the primary researcher for this biography, so I had been hearing updates on its progress for a long time. With these tools, and some earlier collaborative books Milton had published, I would have a better understanding of the work's scope as a resource in my deliberations.

Milton's method of documenting people and places—recording them the way they wanted to be remembered—was my key to finding words. I was interested in, for lack of a better phrase, the mise en scène of the images, the places the subjects had chosen to be photographed and the manner in which they chose to inhabit those environments. These images were the antitheses of formal studio portraiture manipulation. Here, no professional doctoring had taken place. The subjects posed where they wanted, in places that held some meaning for them, and in clothes they wished to represent them, in clothes that reflected daily life, not formal occasions. I understood Milton's aesthetic choice after reading the biography, *Milton Rogovin—The Making of a Social Documentary Photographer*, and came to understand the way Milton's life had been turned upside down, at the hands of others. He had been accused in newspapers of being "Buffalo's Biggest Red," in the hideous chapter of this country's history now referred to as the period of "McCarthyism." Milton was keenly, intimately, aware of the ways others manipulated lives and images toward their own goals. His understanding, I am sure, informed the kinds of relationships he developed with his subjects.

Like the Two Row Wampum that defines the relationship between the Haudenosaunee and the United States, sharing space in tandem, Milton's work did not interfere with the lives of his subject. Consequently, my work also could complement, but never interfere, never presume to speak for what was already so eloquently stated by the images themselves. The initial pieces were to accompany this series' first mounting, but there were specific challenges to the process. I had to wait for the curators to select the images they wanted for the show, and only then could I begin work in earnest. As a result, three poems in the show were pieces I had already written, for another collection. Fortunately, they were still suited to the work. It was as if these poems had been written with the images in mind: the corn, always the corn. Braided, accenting natural design, it was hoisted amid rigid manmade beams, and then, its husks manipulated by a woman into dolls, a longstanding tradition in the culture. This plant gives sustenance and art, passion and nourishment, simultaneously, in harmony. The one new piece grew out of the couple in the "Hendrix Series," inadvertently defining their love, disregarding the fury of popular culture as their backdrop. All of these images are about synthesis and interconnection.

There were many more photos in Milton's collection for which I could have written accompanying poems, had curatorial decisions been made earlier, but time ran out. However, the show was well-received and the opportunity of this book project re-opened the examination of this dialogue. Sorting through the large body of work, I realized there were two distinct, separate bodies, images taken on reservations and images taken in the city of Buffalo. In some significant ways, that separation tended to dictate other aspects of the work. I was intimately familiar with both types of settings. I had grown up at the Tuscarora reservation, and moved to the city when I went to college. At this point in my life, I have, by a few years, lived longer in the city than on the reservation, but I return often, to spend time with family and friends. Tuscarora's place in the Haudenosaunee confederacy is slightly anomalous, in that the nation joined the confederacy in 1724, a long time ago now, but still, a long time after the confederacy's origins. The Senecas had initially been the predominant nation in this area and remain so, to this day, as the living culture continues to reflect its history. The primary architecture of the Haudenosaunee is the longhouse, a rectangular building with an eastern door, a central fire, and a western door. Used initially for living, it is now largely used ceremonially and socially. Because of its significance, some cultural iconography reflects this building's structure. An organizing Haudenosaunee idea is that the territory is one giant metaphoric longhouse. In this view of the territory, Mohawks guard and live at the Eastern Door, Onondagas tend the Central Fire and Senecas keep the Western Door. Initially, the Cayugas and Oneidas were inside, and eventually, the Tuscaroras were added as well.

I was keenly aware of this aspect of our shared culture when realizing a quality of Milton's body of work. Though the two sets of images were shot in the same period of time, the Longhouse's Western Door of Seneca reservation culture was distinctly different from the lifestyles of Buffalo's Lower West Side, the neighborhood many people migrated to when their families left the more rural reservation homes. In seeing that relationship, I had a new and clearer lens on the work. Consequently, I had a better sense of culling a consistent and thematically truthful narrative for this work, without making too many assumptions about specific people within the photos. Now, with the images chosen, I have gone back, with the same stance I had before, trying to find that space where these photos and these poems will run parallel lines, as equals, informing each other and sharing space, alive in their tension and grace—two rows defining themselves and each other.

—Eric Gansworth
July, 2008

What the Photographer Said

Nothing.

Being called
in front of the House
Un-American Activities
Committee, taking the Fifth,
risking livelihood and family
knowing the power of voice
and the power of silence
are two points
on the same line,
he said
nothing.

Branded "Top Red
in Buffalo," by the news,
he picks up a camera
and only then says: "My voice
was essentially silenced,
so I decided to speak
out through photographs."

"The rich have their
photographers," he offers
by way of explanation, pauses,
continues, "I photograph
the forgotten
ones."

It should be
no wonder that Buffalo's Top
Red would wander through
that Western Door to the Lower
West Side, his "red" subjects coming
into focus, unlike Edward Curtis's,
willing, posing, arranging themselves
in their homes, surrounded
by the belongings that shape
their lives and histories, smiling.

Remembered.

Dusk to Dusk

And the way some people tell
our Creation Story, after he covers
the dirt on the turtle's back with grass,
the Good Mind grows
a sunflower next to his lodge,
as a means of lighting
his small place in the world
embracing the state of his needs,
modest to a fault.

Of course, because the story leaves
some aspects of itself open
to interpretation or maybe leaves
holes where details are irrelevant,
we don't know how he comes to grow
the plant here. Did he find
the seeds in the folds
of his grandmother's dress
the way some tell it, the seeds
she carried unknowingly from her place
in the world before this one,
or did he will them into existence
with the strength of his need?
In the world in this time,
things like this are still possible.

And when his place to live
needs little, this flower
is enough for him to find
his way home, lighting
his doorway for some distance.

And when the world grows
too big for the meager ambitions
and good intentions of the flower,
as we all know our worlds
become, despite our own efforts
and intentions, the Good Mind
is offered a solution from the sky.

His grandmother's Elder Brother,
waiting in the clouds for recognition
says he will burn brightly,
attaching himself to the underside
of the Skydome and travel its surface
every day, spreading light for hours
then allowing for darkness to seep in
and govern the sky, balancing his movement.

The Good Mind, in appreciation,
acknowledges that the sunflower
will remain in his doorway,
and with its head, follow the path
the Elder Brother travels
across the sky, sharing light
and the possibilities of life
for every growing thing
on this turtle's back.

And when I think this story
has less and less connection
to me and the places I have lived
and the way the sun traces its arc
away from us and then back again,
a promise kept every day, I remember

a friend's garden, and the haphazard
pattern of sunflowers, like constellations
in the rich soil, and I asked,
in the setting sun, when the flowers bowed
their heads in rest and resignation,
why he had grown them that way.

He said he had grown a couple sunflowers
the previous year, because he liked
watching the way they observed
the sky's daily history, but it turned
out the birds loved the sunflower
as much as he did, perhaps more.

And in taking seeds
from the flower's heart
to feed themselves and likely
their young, they dropped some
along the way, that he neglected
to notice until they were grown
tall enough to be identified,

and as he had come here
from another place, himself,
he knew the way seeds could fall
in places they had not expected
and still survive, growing
into the beings they were intended
to be, chasing the sun
from a different point
beneath the sky, sending seeds
themselves when the time came.

What the Photographer Saw

Two places separated by forty miles,
an ambitious day's journey by foot
reduced to less than an hour
with cars and a highway, two places,
where the roads could hardly be
more different from one another,

the first, dirt paths
in rolling hills and family
farm patches, worn to roads
by generations of feet
and eventually paved
into the twentieth century
where driveways left impressions
of the time before, and residents
accepted mud as a way of life
in some seasons of the year

the second, measured, blocked
and orderly, an urban grid in place,
at least on a drawing board
before that long walk from homes
where babies were born
on the kitchen table, to this
place where those calloused hands
become the limbs of balancing artists
who would construct the iron-skeletons
of this place they would grow
to call home, maybe forgetting
the ploughed fields in years,
favoring the dotted-lined

streets, whose turns could be
predicted every few yards.

He saw what remained
and he saw what was left.

A man who keeps doing
what his family has done
for more generations
than his collective relatives
have the capacity to remember.

He saw the ways the man prepared
for the tougher seasons
when the earth was less willing
to offer its gifts to those
who don't want to work for them.

In fields and yards, he saw
trees transformed to cordwood
low walls built between house
and outhouse, a fortress wall
in October, reduced to a hint
of a wall by May, when doors opened
wide to let in sun and breeze

and trees celebrated, whittled
and carved into snow snakes,
to embrace the knowledge
that winter, even as it forces

the world to sleep, offers
us different pleasure,
sliding the carved wood length
down a frozen path to test
the strength and agility
of the thrower and the grace
and nuance of the carver.

And he saw what remained
and he saw what was left.

He saw where, for some
the rituals of home
had been whittled,
like snow snakes,
into something else
entirely, something sleek.

He saw an Indian man
and an African-American man
in a dimly lighted
wood-paneled room,
meeting each other
on a floor cleared
for the art of dancing,
linoleum masquerading
as tile spreading
across the floor
like a perspective drawing

where the speakers separating
them on the floor, filled with sound
and inspiration, suggest
the only drums in this room
are recorded, a backbeat
for a different kind of movement,
a different kind of song,
a different kind of dance,
a different kind of social,

and this is where they discover
themselves and each other

where the cordwood is absent,
and the dividing walls
are so consuming
that even the windows
are covered with brick,
implying the world
inside and the world
outside are not so good
for the future of either,

where the message left
for anyone wandering lost
in this particular territory
housed within the borders
of the Western Door

are asked to think
of the parallel histories
of Wounded Knee
and Attica and
if they are not sharp
enough to draw
their own conclusions,
one has been provided
sprayed onto the permanency
of these bricks piled
on one another,
sealed with mortar
and blood.

Harvest and Germination

After the harvest,
when the corn has dried
and the bee convened
to braid the ears
into long strands,
and we cough from the dust
raised in the braiding,
we smile, sore-handed
and stiff-jointed, because
we know there will be corn,

and though someone might find
this corn not to their taste,
the way it is lyed and washed,
lyed and washed, transformed,
and though they might think it
a food of desperation,
we know different, as we hoist
the braids to the barn beams
in preparation for the dark
months of winter
and their uncertain
days of food from other
places, that when we taste
this food, watching ice-crystals
spread across the windows
like locusts, that this
is the taste of familiarity,
the taste of comfort and history
the taste of dreams past
and dreams future,
the taste of home.

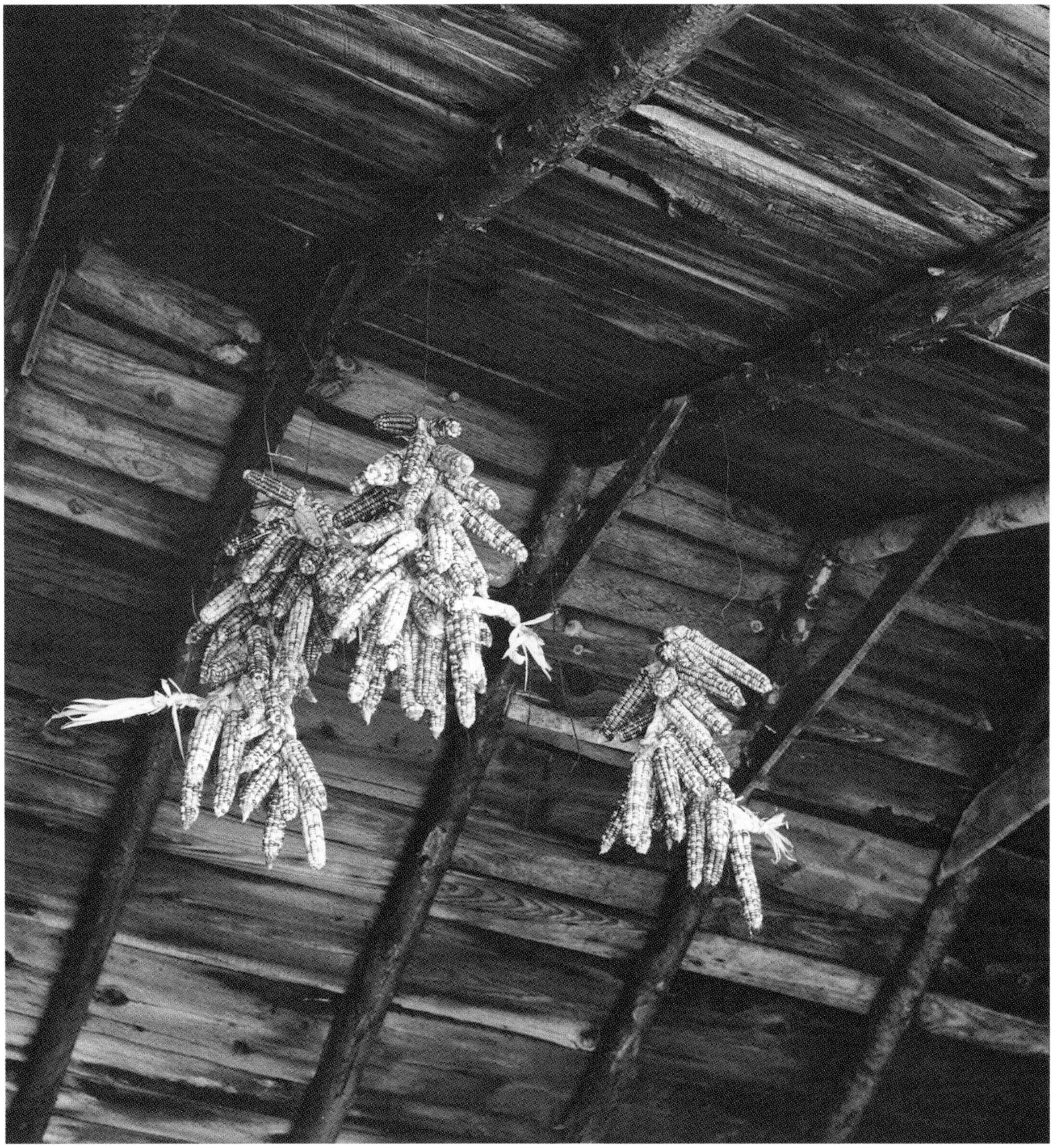

Her Creations

She gathers them in her arms
holding them as she might
an infant, or a child
that government agents
might suggest would be better
served by a boarding school
away from home and away
from family, and everything
else that keeps them
from successfully moving
into this other world.

These small, faceless people,
naked as the day any of us
is born, are yet to be shaped
by time and circumstance
into something more explicit
and unadorned as they are,
she understands the belief
that we are not supposed to draw
faces on their blank heads.

Any mark left behind
by another hand is a trace
of responsibility for the future
directions for all involved,
and she stands in the doorway
holding them close
in ways her children
no longer allow her
to do, for it becomes clear
when the photographer pulls back

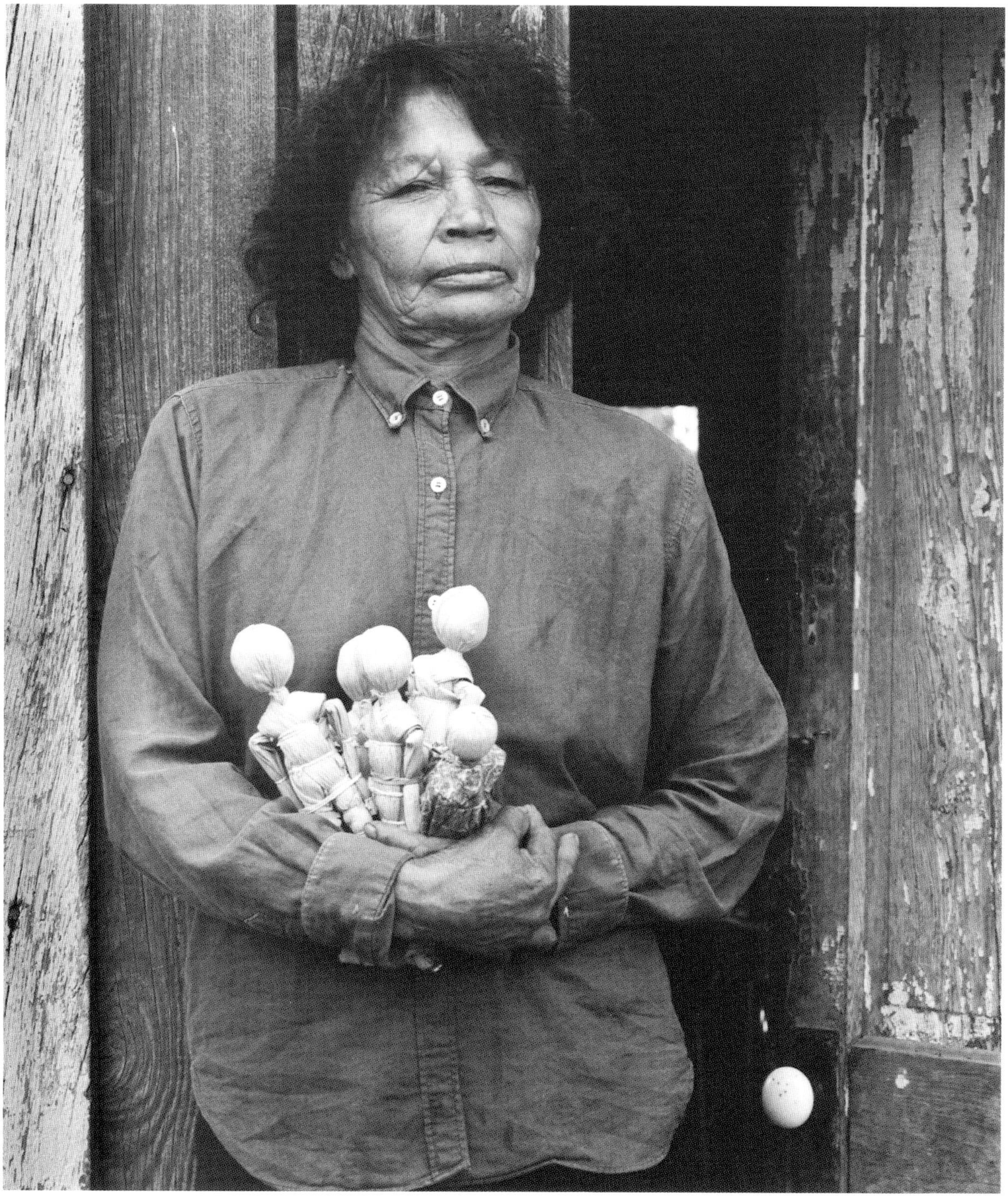

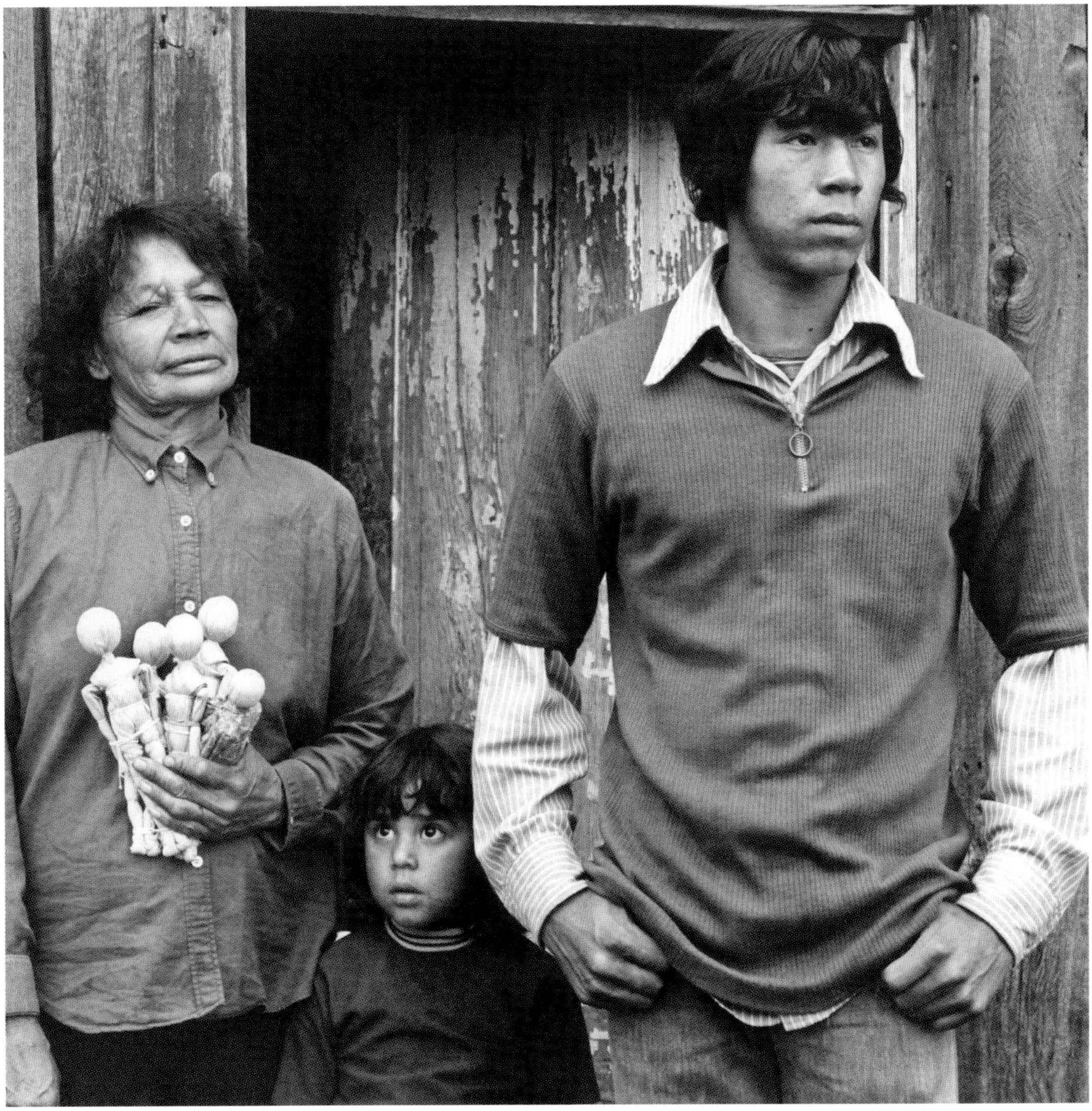

and we see other glimpses
of her life as it is
at that moment. The doorway
reveals shadows from within
the house where she has raised
a family. Walking out of it,
her real children are marked
already by the world outside,
ignoring her workclothes, unadorned,
favoring wide collars and zippered pullovers
that would have placed them anywhere beyond
a farm where cornhusks are readily available
to be shaped by loving imagination.

They look away from their mother
and the gifts she offers, as if
it were nothing to conjure beauty
from the scraps left after harvest,
and she knows they stare out
into a future where they live
some other place and begin
shaping their own imaginations,
leaving her here with the husks
and the dreams she kindled,
for herself and for them.

She hopes, as they leave, they will
remember, when they grow hungry for home
at some day down the road,
in their other, unforeseen place,
that Indian corn can only come

from a previous year's growth,
and that care needs to taken,
to ensure future harvest fields,
if they are, when they decide,
ready and able to carry on.

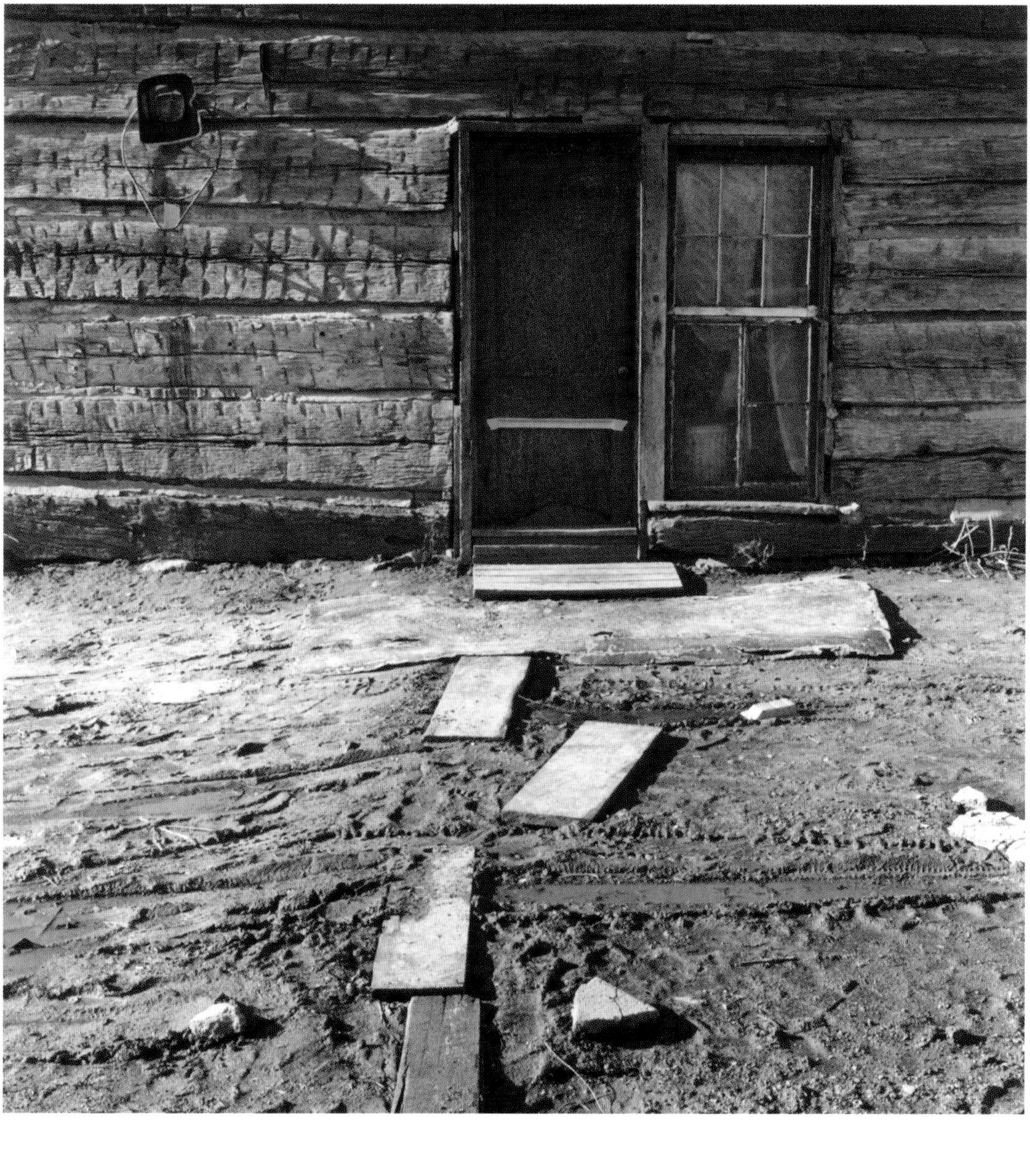

The Grandmothers

And so we name the moon
for them, as they mark our days
weeks, months, and years,
in the trace of our shadows
across their faces,
and we come to accept
the ways they draw us in
and send us out, we are their tides
their wakes, our every move
dictated by the pull
of their cycles.

This same moon shines
in the dark for all of us,
chasing the Elder Brother sun
from the Western Door
to the Lower West Side,
across these lines in the dirt
where we make our imprints
until the end of our days.

When we leave the earth
and rain washes our tracks
from the places we've been,
it is her arrivals we count,
the ten appearances of her face
in the night sky before we send you to her
with a feast for your journey.

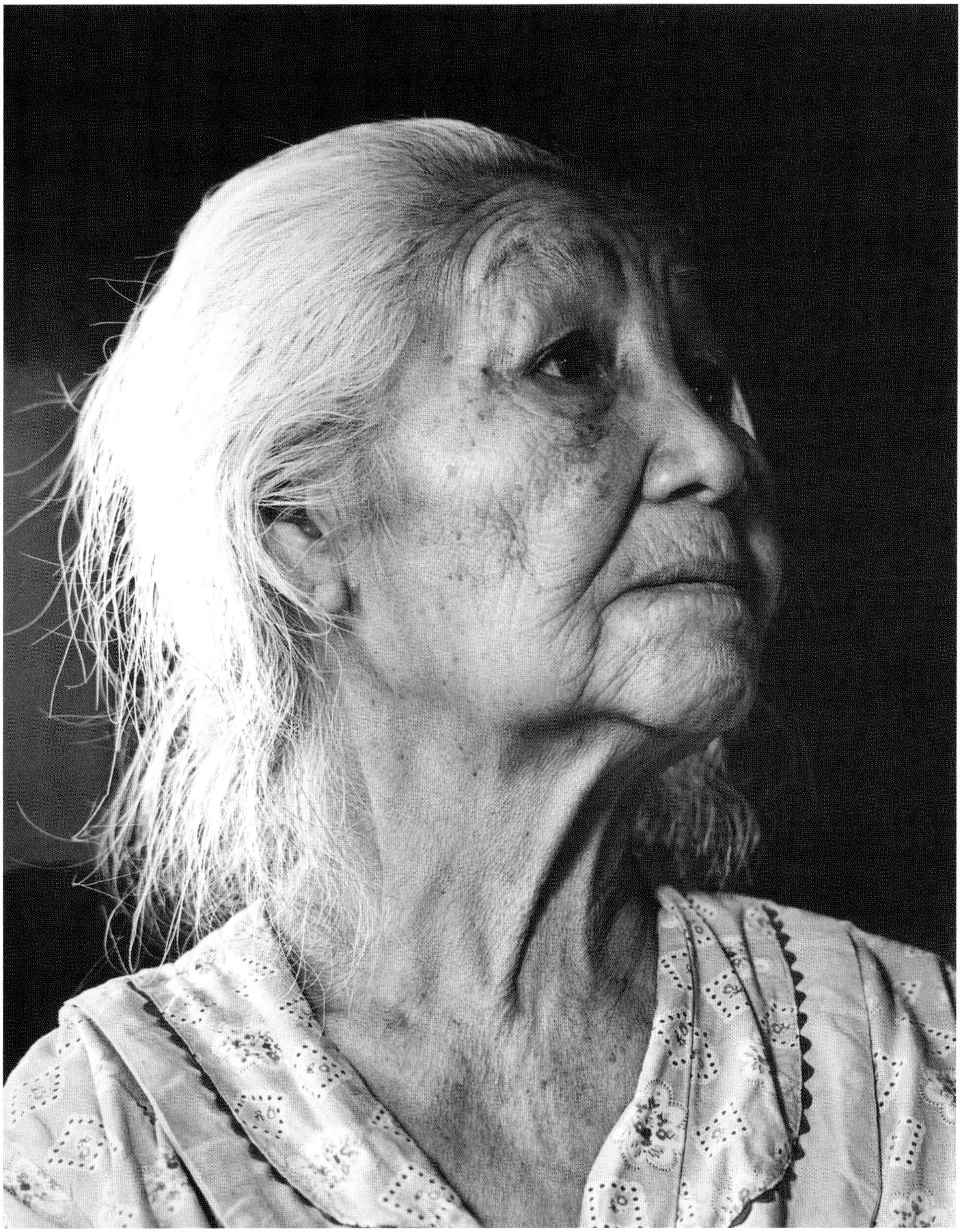

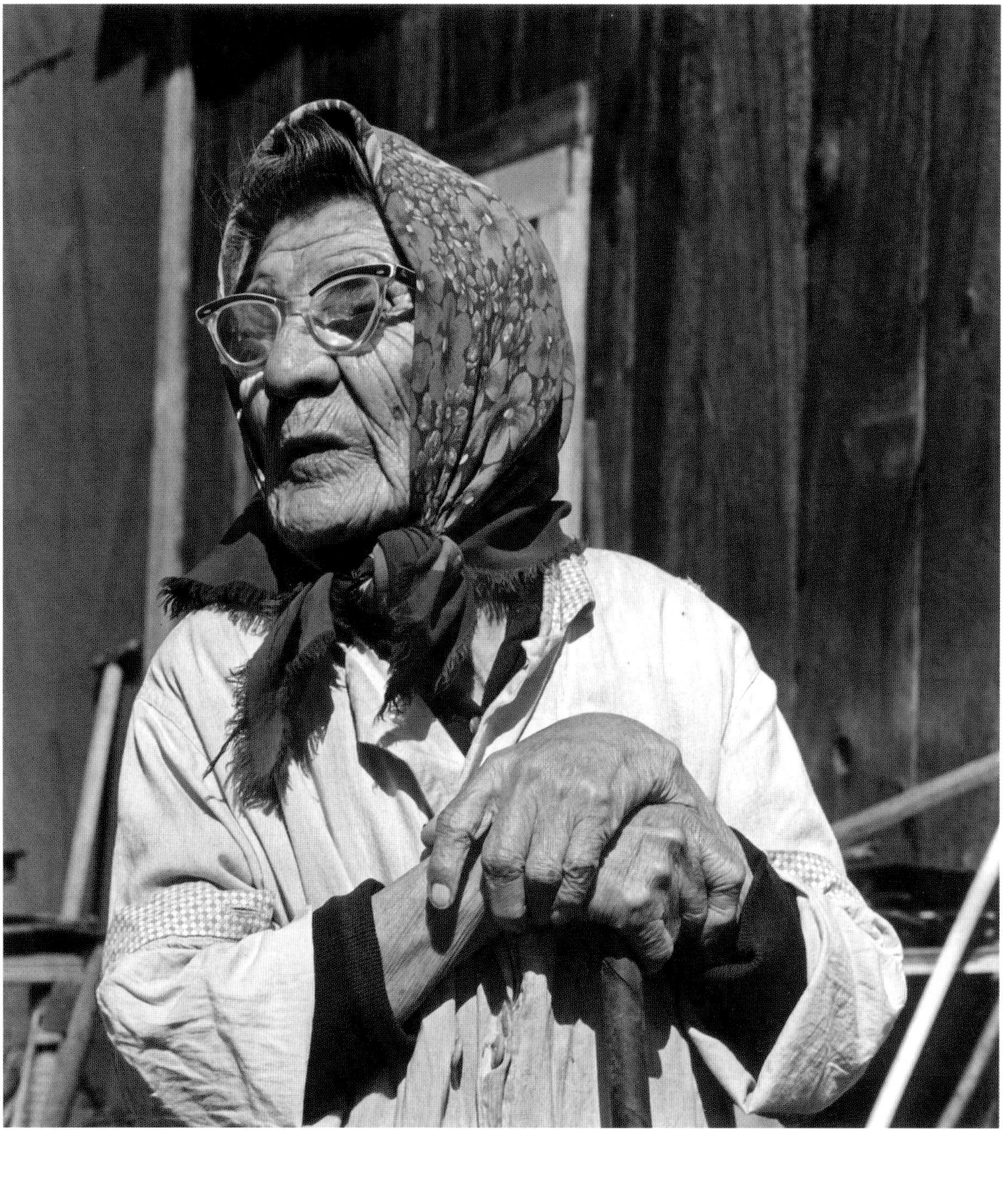

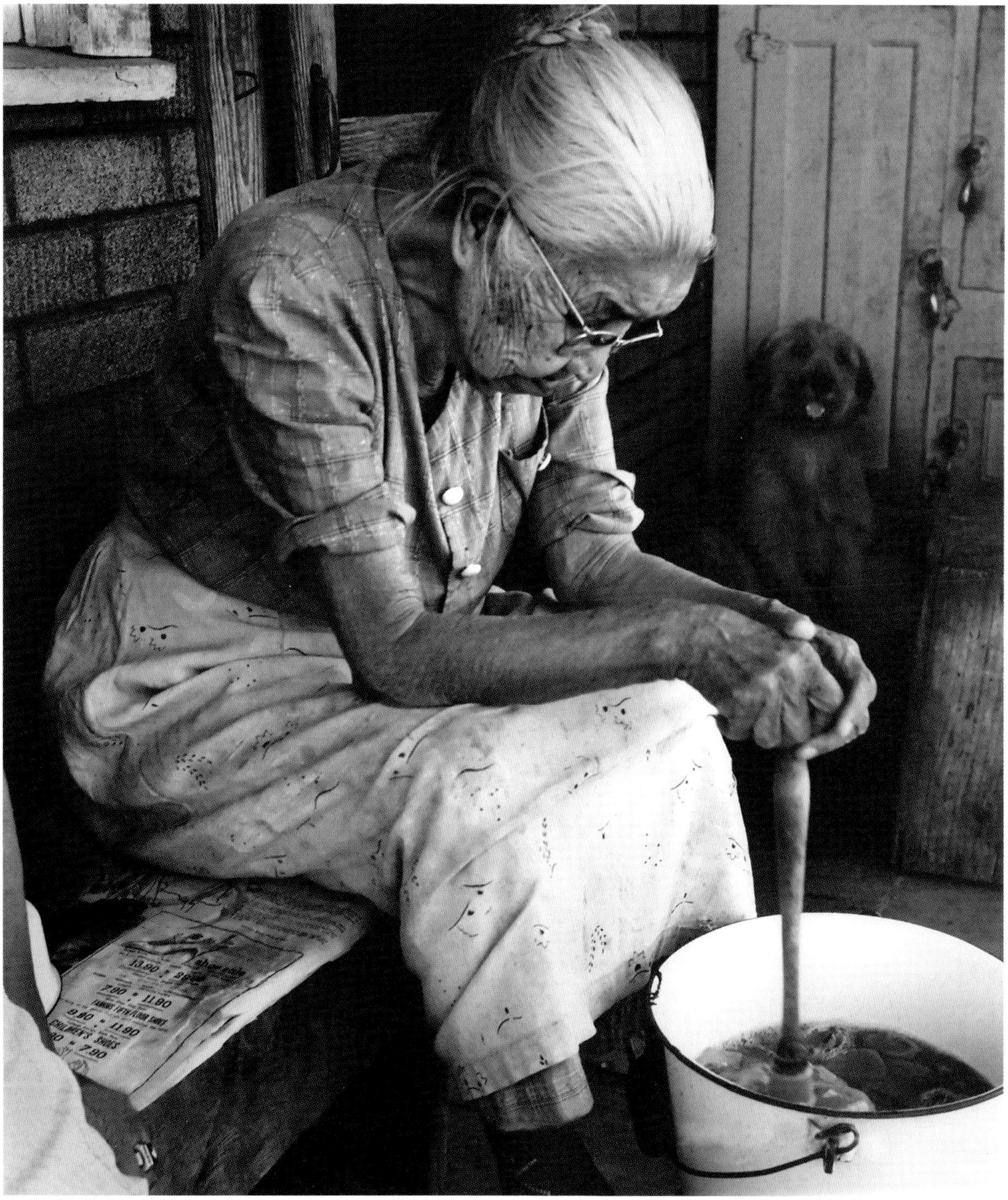

And while we are still here
when we lose that life in the city
among the orderly grids and street lights
and the 24 hour stores with chain links
covering their windows,
and the check cashing
places and the pawn shops,
and homes stacked one upon another
that we pay someone else to inhabit,
we will head back home

where the roads have no yellow lines
dotted or solid, dividing them
and the smell of wet earth
and wood smoke replace
the clouds of sewer
and diesel and gas fumes,

where the driveways
are made of mud
and ruts and planks
salvaged from houses gone
to ground,

where maybe the walls and roofs
fail, and the paint peels,
and the wells dry, and the electricity
is shut off for lack of payment,

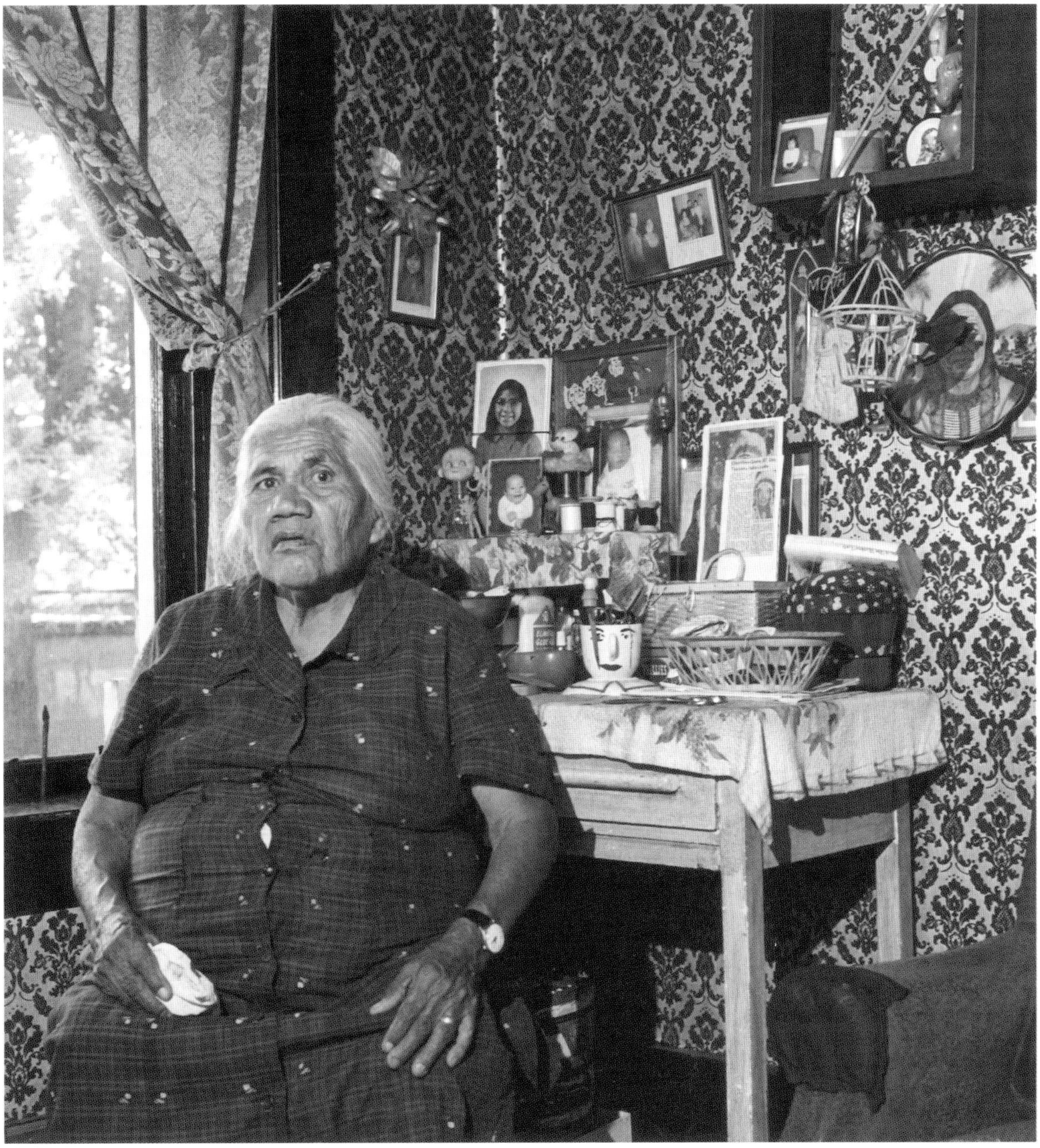

there, we find
these grandmothers, who
were first defined by the Elder
Woman's face in
the night sky.

To remind us who she is
we only need look around
these houses where we were born
and raised, and the women,
ever present, who keep going
and going.

We give thanks to her
and eventually join her
after a life well lived.
Her company is our reward, and
this is what we understand
about our grandmother,
the moon.

WOUNDED KNEE
ATTICA
WOUNDED KNEE
ATTICA
WOUNDED KNEE
ATTICA
ATTICA
PATRIA
O
MUERTE
LA
LUCHA
SIGUE

Baby Picture

Before they take on that role
the grandmothers allow us glimpses
along the lines of seven
generations. They are
first infants, babies, almost
indistinguishable from one
another, dark shifting forms
laughing and crying,
moving in the ways of
freedom they dictate,
knowing in that secret place
that they will carry us through.

They wriggle on the laps of others
who've already made tracks
between these two places, and
maybe farther, but who always
come back, family stretching
and growing too sprawling
to fit inside the viewfinder
of the photographer who
appears every few years
to mark the progress
of their tendrils into this world.

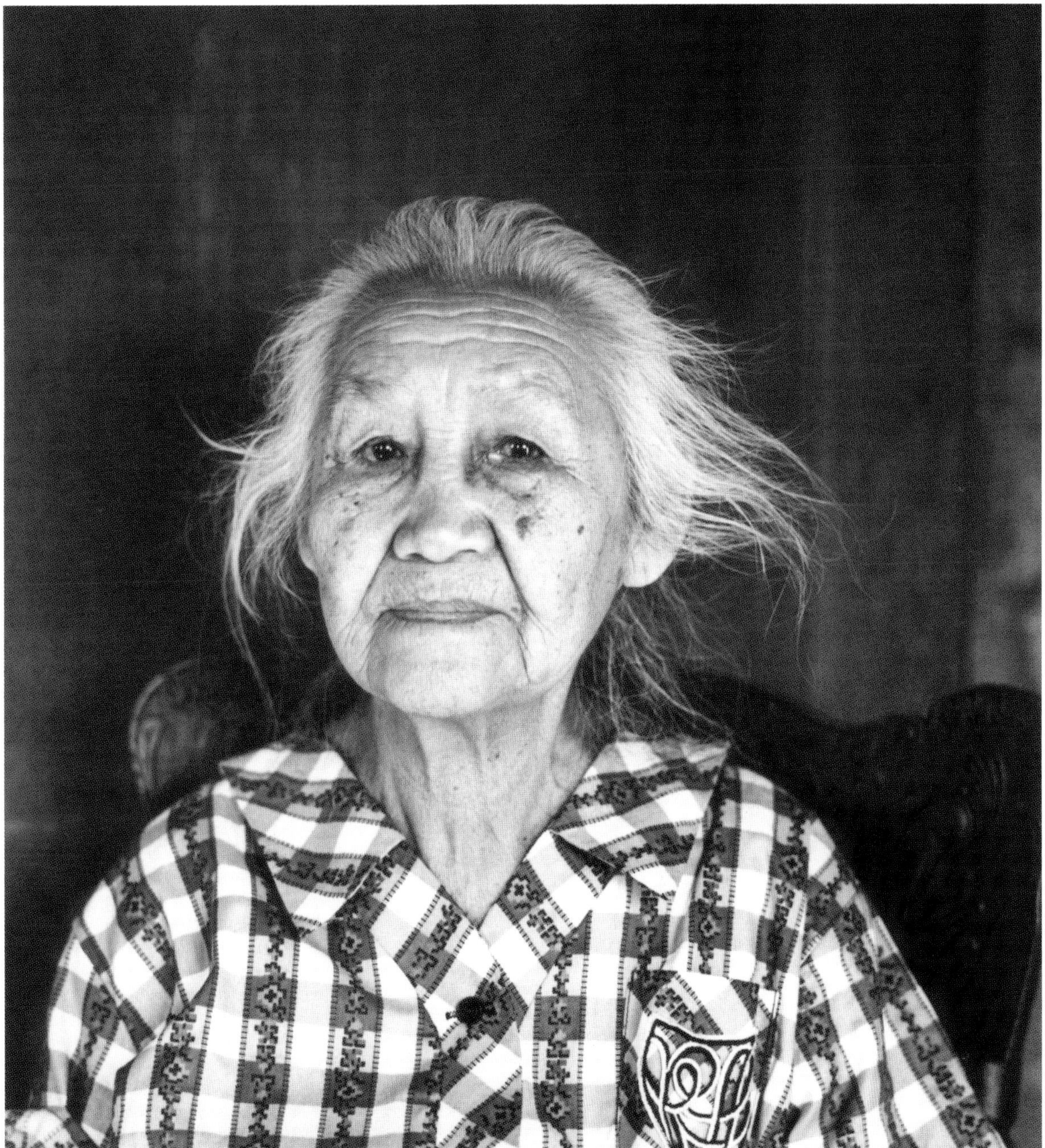

And here, in these arms, they are
frozen for a moment, and one day
generations from now, some
young girl, sharing the same DNA,
learning to speak
well enough to inherit
the responsibility of stories
will point a familiar finger at
a baby in the photograph
who looks like her and ask
after its identity.

And the mother, holding the girl
and the photo will say:
"That is your grandmother,"
asserting the connection anew.

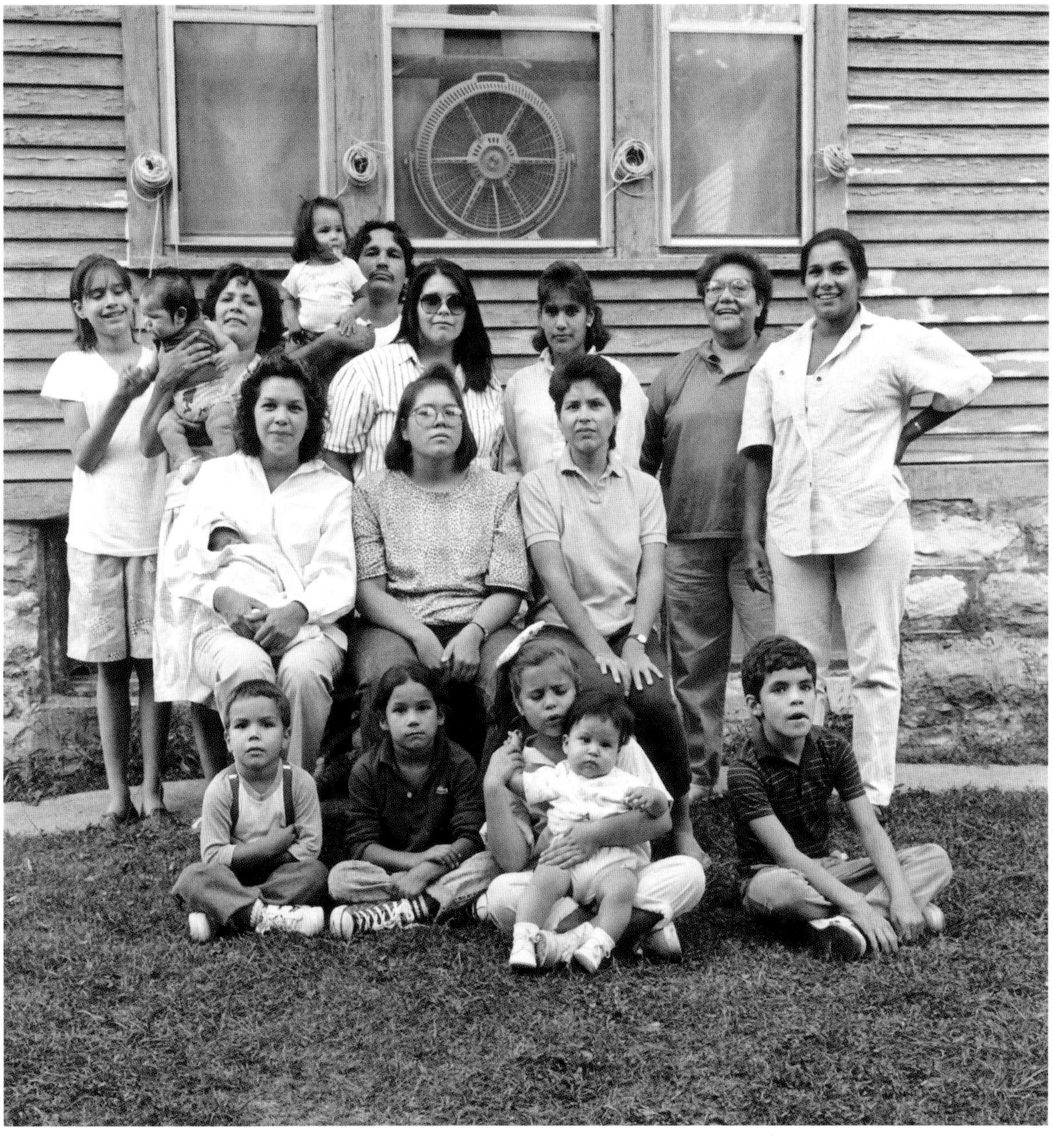

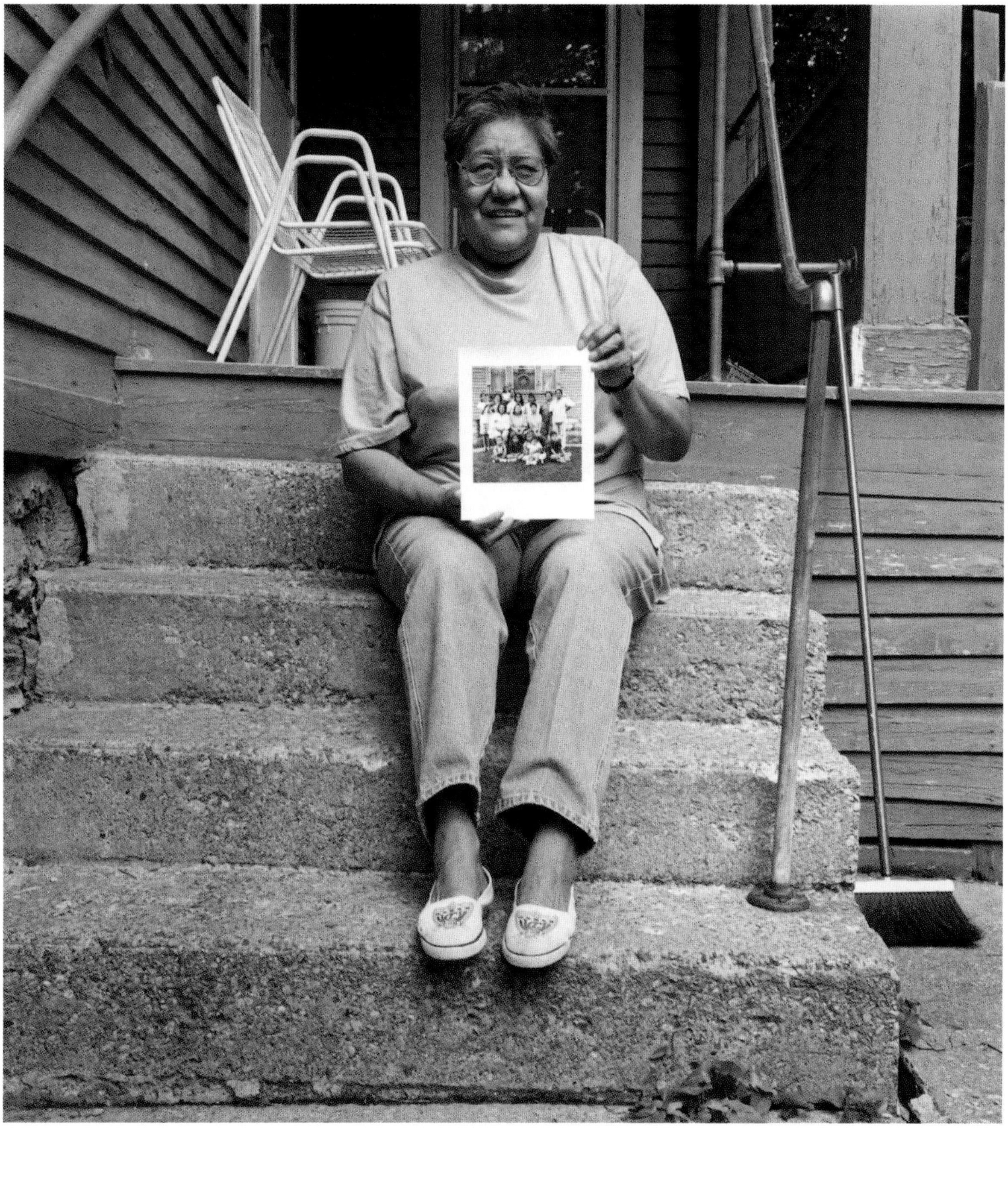

Family Connection, Once Removed

She holds this photo, smiling, tentative,
as if it were crystal, ready to shatter
leaving only blood and loss in her hands,
this image of the squirming babies
on the laps of their mothers, surrounded
by aunts, uncles, cousins, before a house
where a fan forces outside air
among their belongings
demanding they breathe in and breathe
out, and they will one day become
grandmothers enduring, as she herself does,

on an urban porch, lawn chairs
behind her at a city home where
there is no lawn for them, and she is framed
by another door, and a railway guiding her
into the street, but she's stopped here,
in Levi's and a T-shirt on the third step
of cast concrete,
joining her family
in the only way
she can at that moment.

And though this is the city removed,
removed, are those beaded moccasins
on her feet, and if not,
can we say they are
with the same conviction
she uses to hold on?

Three More Sisters

Corn and Beans and Squash
removed from the mounds
where we planted them
together, relying on
their collective strengths,
learn to grow
in tougher soil.

They find themselves
and each other
working days at factories
fingers shrouded in rough gloves
leaving no traces of prints,
names and voices lost
to machine noises
and at night
amid orderly rows
of metal, wood, drywall,
cramped homes stacked one atop
the other, where the sun
might shine through one
or two windows for a couple
hours a day, and the sounds
of others' lives bleed through
these buildings designed to give
the illusion of privacy and safety.

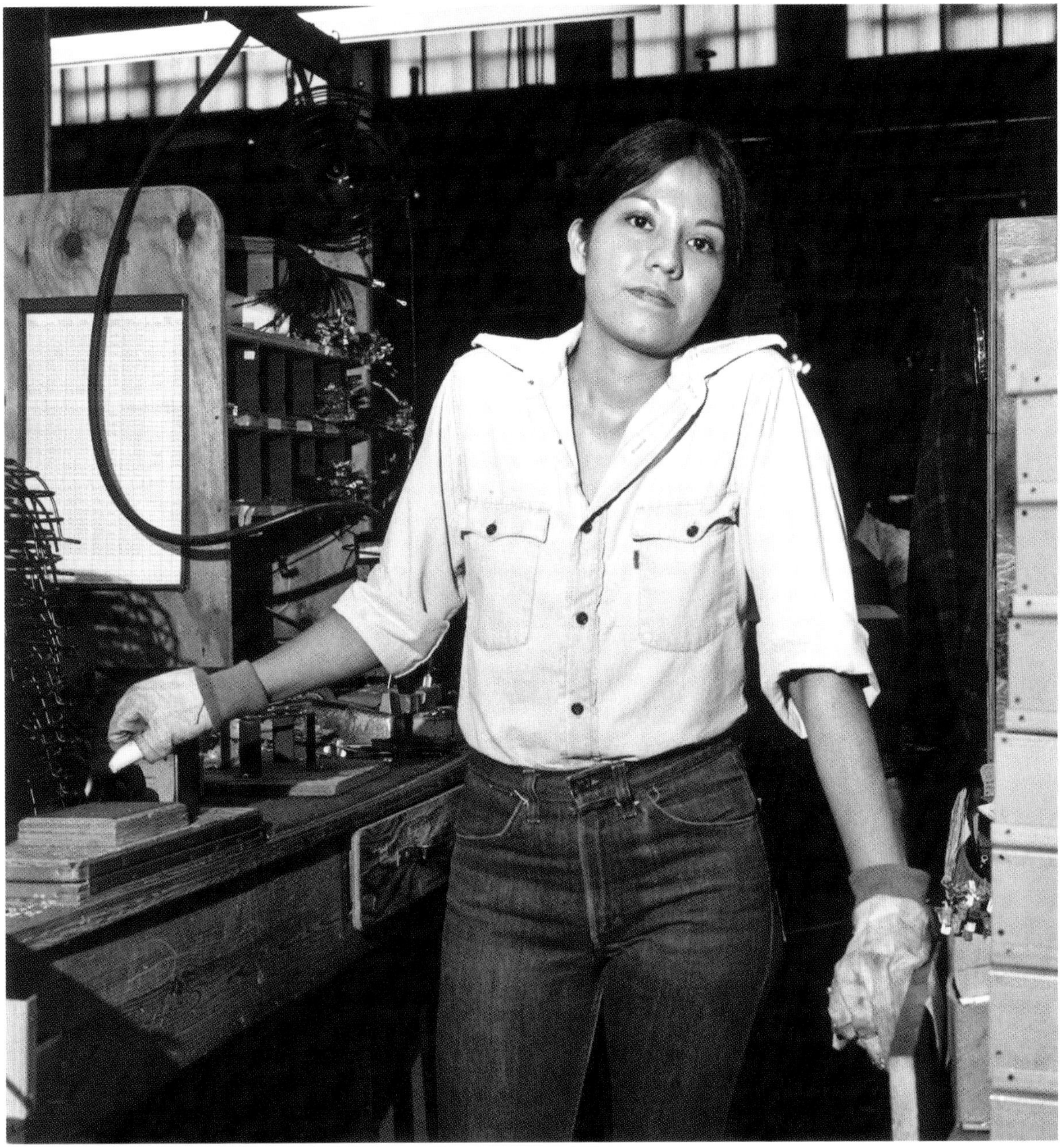

"Maybe," one of them thinks,
listening to things they don't want
to hear in the middle of the night,
smashing glass, arguments, screams
a near miss at a STOP light,
"this is what it was like
in the olden days,
when we lived together
in longhouses, and
there were always
outsiders who drew
us together, reconnecting
re-establishing and
reproducing, growing
stronger in resistance,
like steel tempered
in a firestorm.

Beads

"Hunting
            Fishing
                        Trapping

PROHIBITED"

the sign mounted above
her states, cascading yellowing
authority peeling from the walls,
its top declaration
"Seneca Nation of Indians"
underscored by a cable
television line
snaking above sightlines
in this West Side apartment,
mainlining American
popular culture through
her TV.

Cornered, arms crossed casually
but crossed just the same
she stands guard
between two doors
one opened and one closed.

Seneca Nation of Indians
HUNTING
FISHING
TRAPPING
PROHIBITED

Shelved between them
keeping her company
a bridge holding a series
of tiny, carved elephants
at one end, a tiny
sewing machine at the other.
And mounted to the door frame,
as if needing to be noted
with every movement in
or out, beaded Wolf Clan
and Thunderbird medallions,
while a lone key hangs between them
asking her always,
to remember.

"The earth
and
myself
are
of one
mind."
"Let us put
our minds
together
and see what
life
we will make
for our
children."
THE LONG DEATH
BLACK PEPPER
WONDER

Books

She reads silently at a table
lined with books,
a shelf of condiments
and cooking supplies below it,
the silent Calumet can waiting
for her to make peace
in abstraction and stillness
but she listens instead, to

Sitting Bull, taped to her wall,
peering over her shoulder,
and whenever she dreams
of joining the Calumet contents
as so much powder
drifting across some strange counter
she looks up, and Sitting Bull
repeats, whenever their eyes meet:

"Let us put
our minds
together
and see what
life
we will make
for our
children,"

and she returns to the book
and lamp before her
leaving the Calumet below
the surface, understanding
peace without its benefit.

Beds

Cocooned in patchwork quilts
old dresses and skirts, and shirts,
and any other piece of cloth
no longer useful, cut, rearranged,
sewn back together in a new life,
she disregards the chain and cord
hanging above her like a tether
amid a pillow stripped
naked as she is
and a mattress
whose sheet peels back
beneath her

and she smiles, in bold intimacy,
an accomplishment because you know
our history with blankets, and photographers,
and the things they might carry
our way and leave behind with us.

All you need to know about her smile is
the butterfly of ink scarring her skin
with its wings and flight and
all the ways it is no longer
a caterpillar, inching
across that turtle's back.

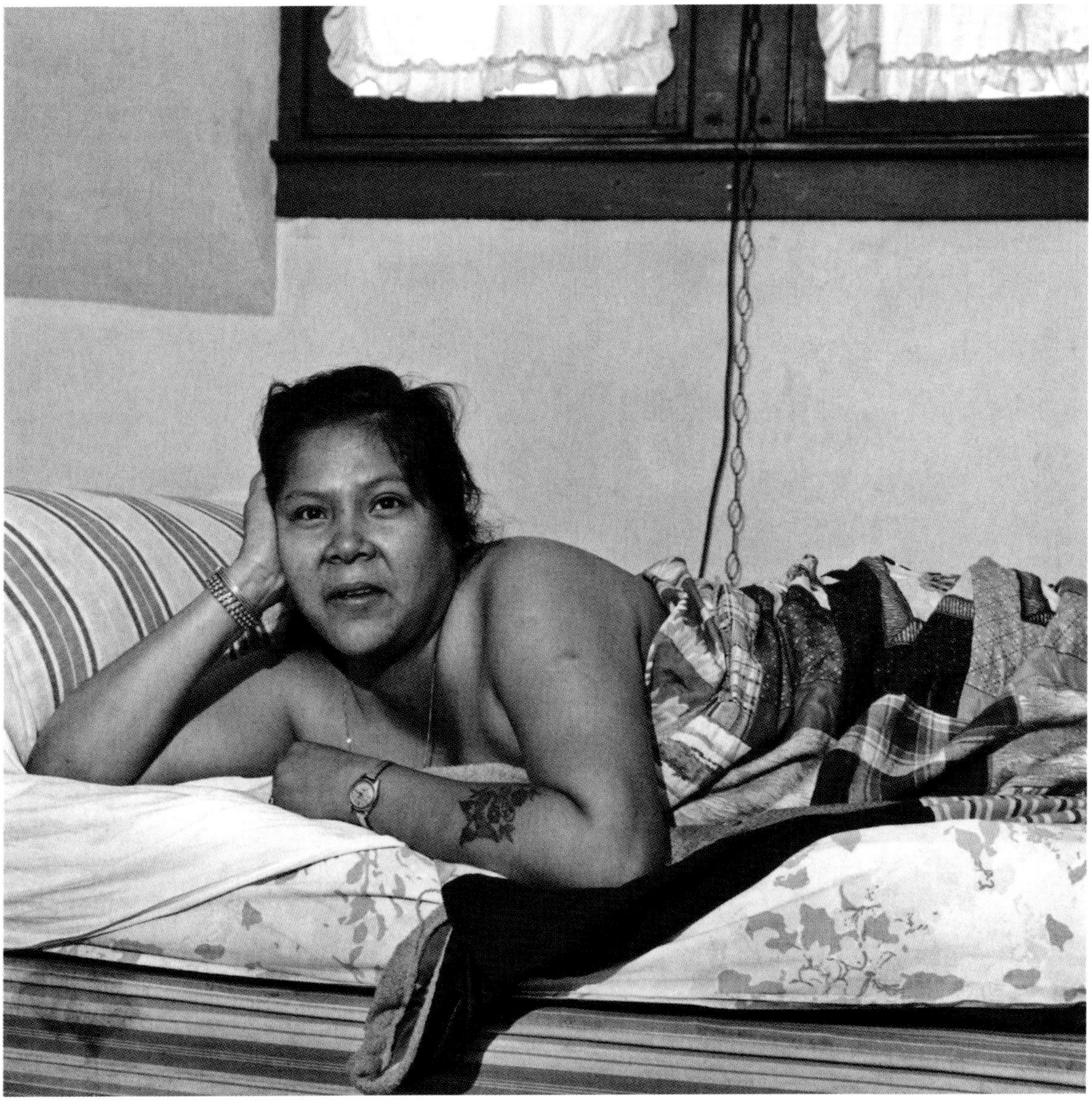

How can you not believe,
in this place where a new generation
will be conceived,
in a new life awaiting you
with the evidence on her forearm
chasing its own
shadows across flowers
in bloom, pollinating
along the way?

While Hendrix Played a Solo: "Burning of the Midnight Lamp"

Above them, locked by thumbtacks
to the walls of a Lower West Side
apartment, ignoring the topless
woman pinned to the next wall,
lighting Monterey on fire with a fret
board and strings and those wondrous
fingers, Jimi filled the night
with a haze so purple it rivaled
the wampum beads these two would know
as surely as their own names,
tracing history, culture,
treaties that mostly document
violation—they knew Purple Haze
in their tissue, organs, blood.

In a chair designed for a single
body, they sat together, Skin to
Skin, she wearing Janis Joplin
glasses to see the world
through, he letting his hair grow
into history and toughening up his bare
soles, for the long haul,
testifying that they were
not like those Indians
Edward Curtis imagined through his lens,
they were not vanishing, not going
anywhere—the West Side still
within the territories
they had guarded for centuries.

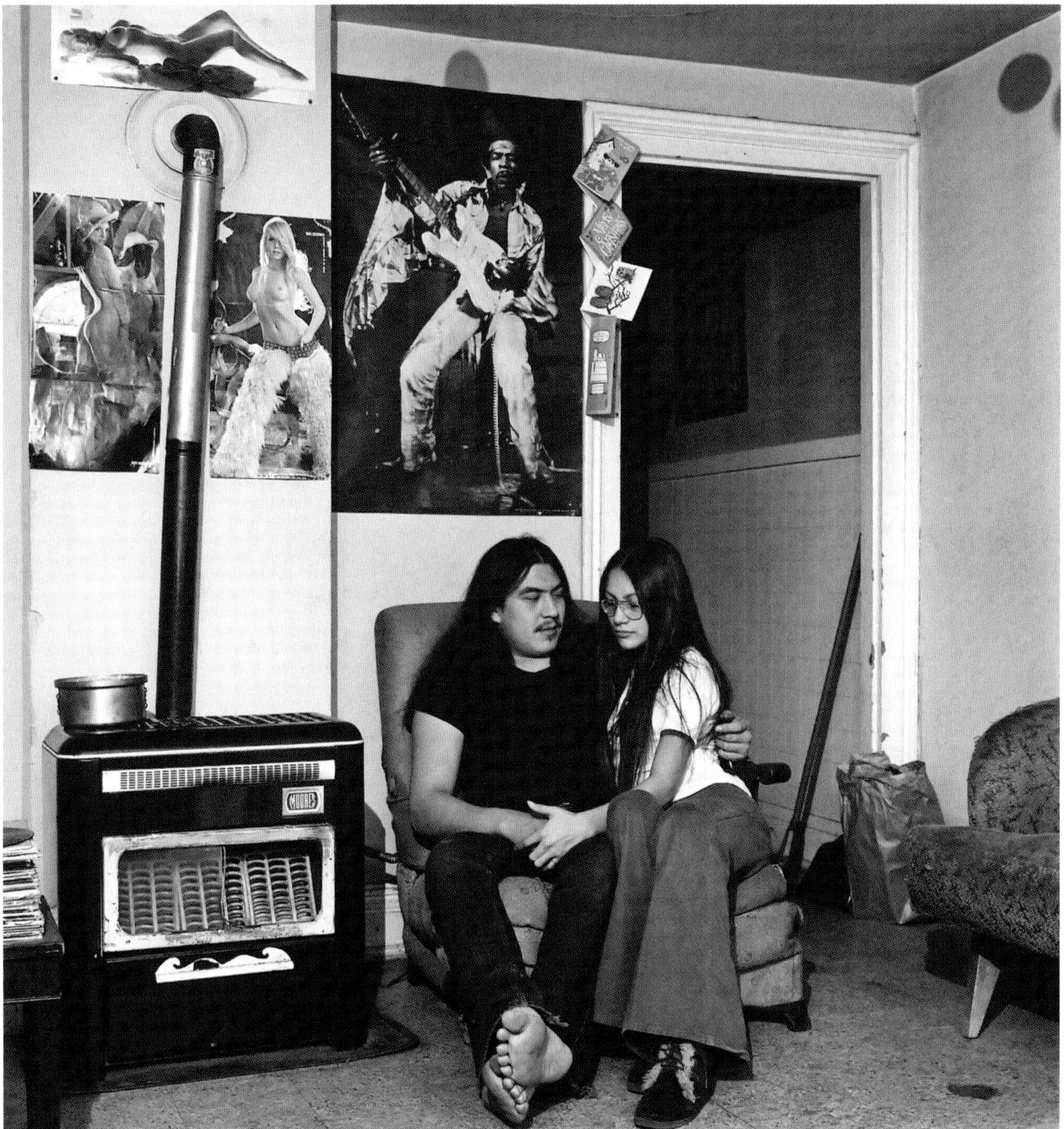

The western door behind
them, they look at one
another, confident before
the photographer, that this is
the way they want to be recognized,
recorded—hand in hand, knowing
as Jimi did, that "The Star
Spangled Banner" could
bring tears to one's eyes
for a variety of reasons
and that their responsibility
was to hang on as all the other
Indians had before them
surviving to tell the tale, together.

While Hendrix Played a Solo: "Gypsy Eyes"

The only things we see of Jimi
are furrowed brow, pumped fist,
the tuned head of his Fender
diminished, as they look this time
into the camera, even head ducked,
cocked to one side, seeming to
look at each other, their eyes
really connect with the camera's lens.

For this moment they do not need
to face one another, look into
each other's eyes, searching
for that truth of commitment.

Jimi might have asked: "Are You
Experienced?" and they could answer
"Yes, We Are," but there is no need
for a caption, word balloons, graffiti.

We can read the way their clothing
complements their lives, familiar, similar,
understated, and we can read the way
four hands touch in arms entwined
and encompassing, a circle
closed to outside influence.

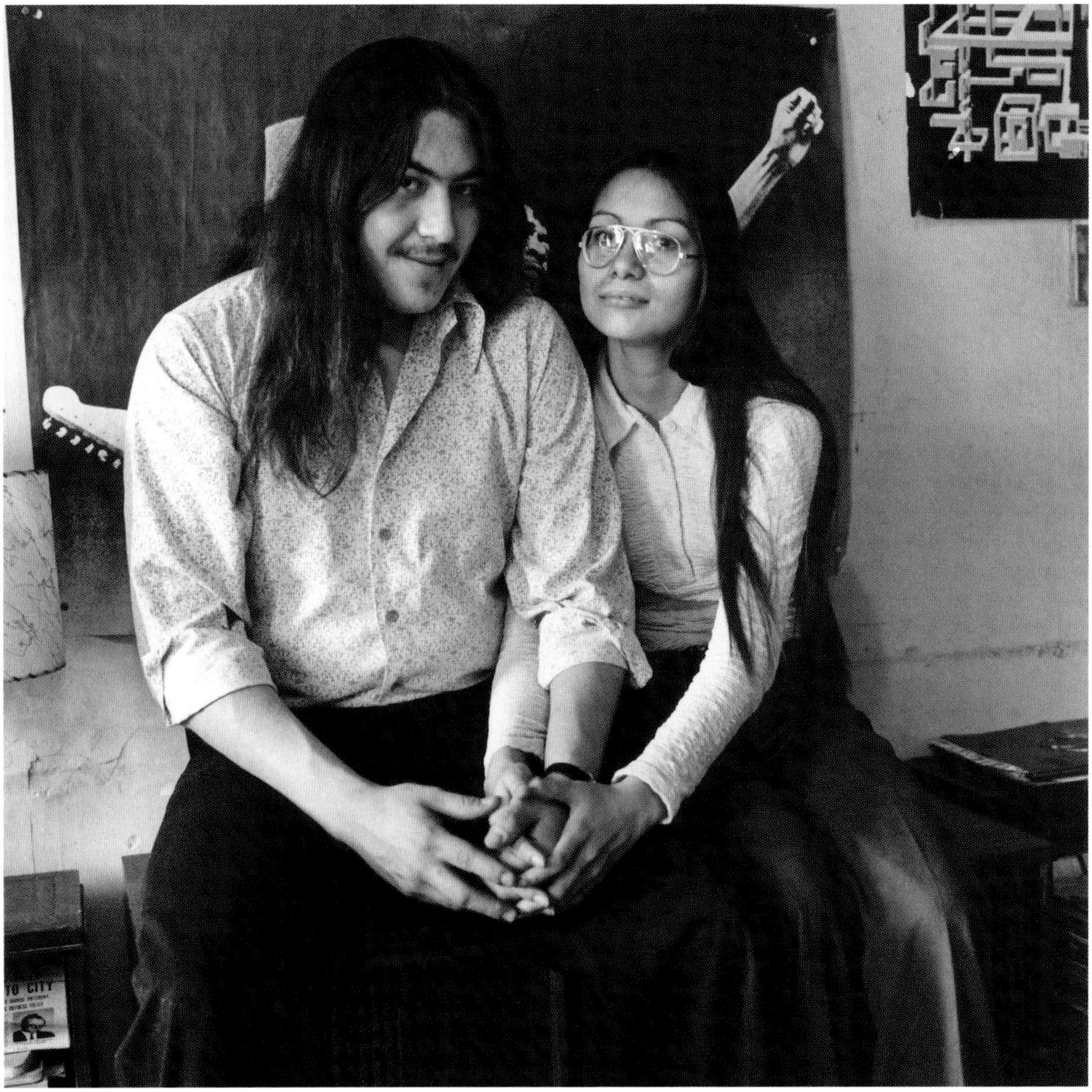

While Hendrix Played a Solo: "Purple Haze"

Years later, against flimsy walls
where the wallpaper ripples
like waves on Lake Erie's shore
or veins coursing through
this Lower West Side apartment,
their couch rests, the urgency
of a shared chair no longer needed.

Their hair is cut, pulled back,
tamed, and they forget
the camera this time,
his one arm thrown casually
against the couch back,
as they both study the place
their hands meet.

The topless women have abandoned
Jimi, left him against the wall alone,
moving on to some other place
softening the ache of some
lonelier heart, replaced
by an electric clock, its cord
streaming reliably, counting
the cycles of years, months,
weeks, days, hours,
minutes and seconds
they have spent together,

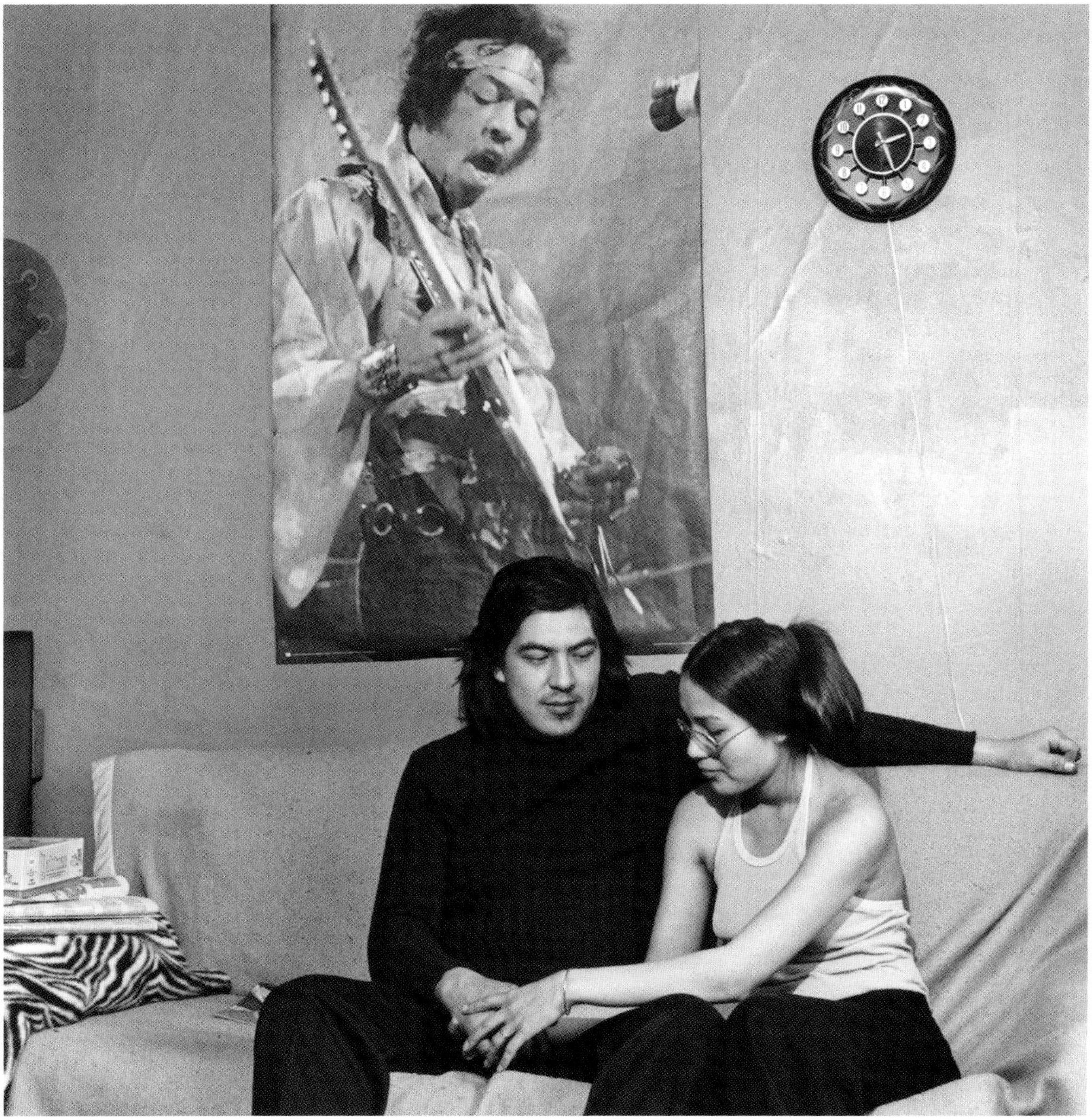

and even from his vantage point
in the night sky above them
as he blazes away on those six strings
filling the air with wampum sounds,
he can't help but notice
the small gleam
of her wedding band,
play them a wedding song,
and stand up as witness for them.

West Side Social

I don't know where
or when this is, so like
that night somewhere
in a church or hall on Elmwood,
that blacktop line separating
the Lower West Side from
Downtown, Allentown, the Chippewa
hot spots, and the tall, cramped
Elmwood houses people call a "village"
in an effort to find a home.

We gathered in that room, filling
its empty chairs with our survivor
bodies, warming ourselves
with cornsoup and frybread
and so much song, those
of us with silent voices
taking in the music
and memory like sunlight
and strawberry drink
on a winter day,

where Kris in Factory Outlet
Reeboks took up
a rattle and cleared
his throat with responsibility
as he always does

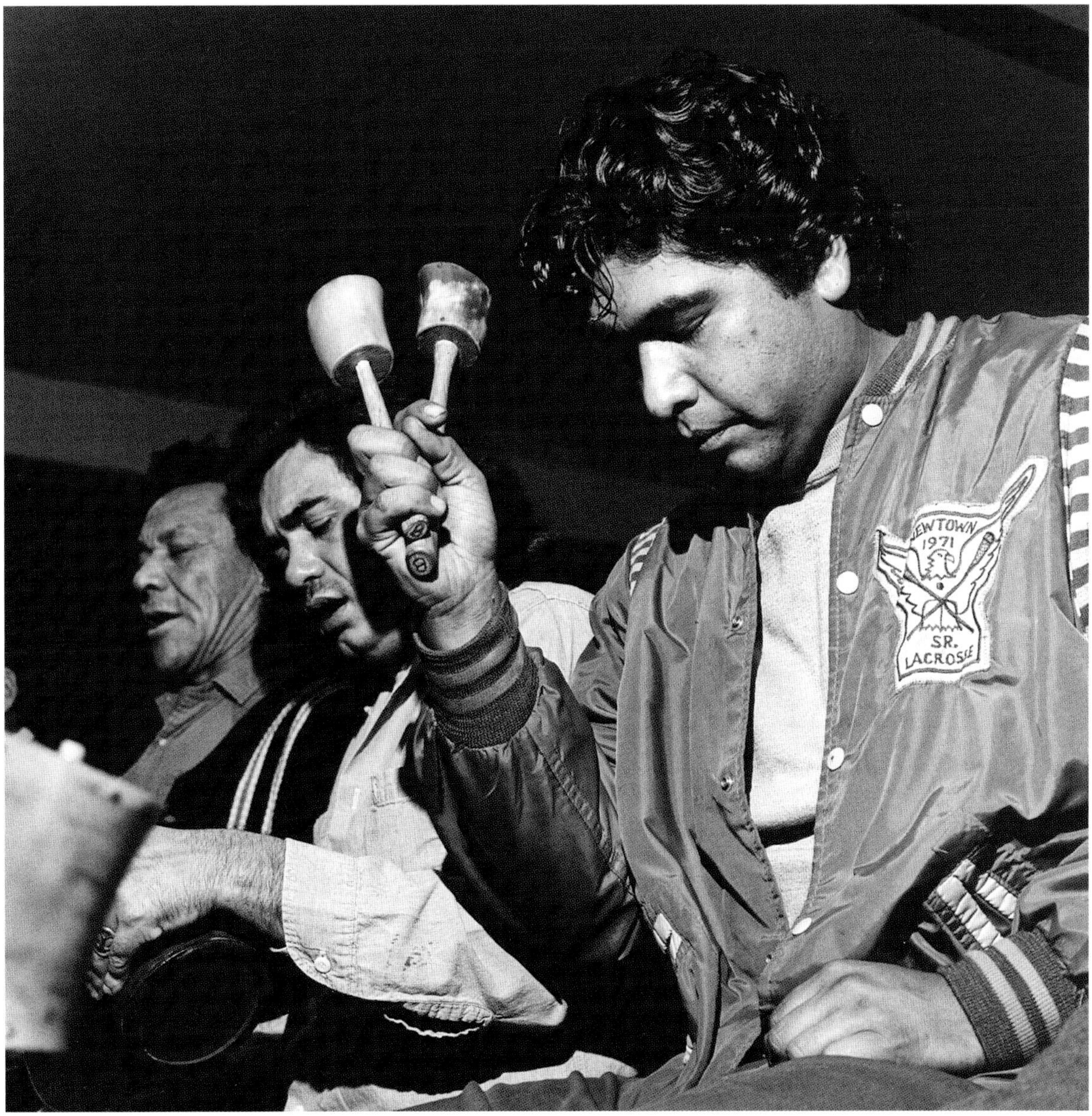
NEWTOWN
1971
SR.
LACROSSE

and Angie, even in
her "hot heels," stepped
out across the varnished wood
floor, skidding as often
as shuffling in those gleaming
patent leather stacked-heel shoes
during the women's dance
that defines our place
on this turtle's back

laughing with those
in moccasins and steel toe
ironwork boots, defining
themselves and us with their feet
pounding our repeating rhythms
of identity and history

so much like these men
and these women and these
elder women and these
elder men, and these
children, young girls and
young boys who will know
how to sing and dance and take
a horn rattle
and a drum and move
body and mind for all
each is worth, with
precision for seven generations
in either direction

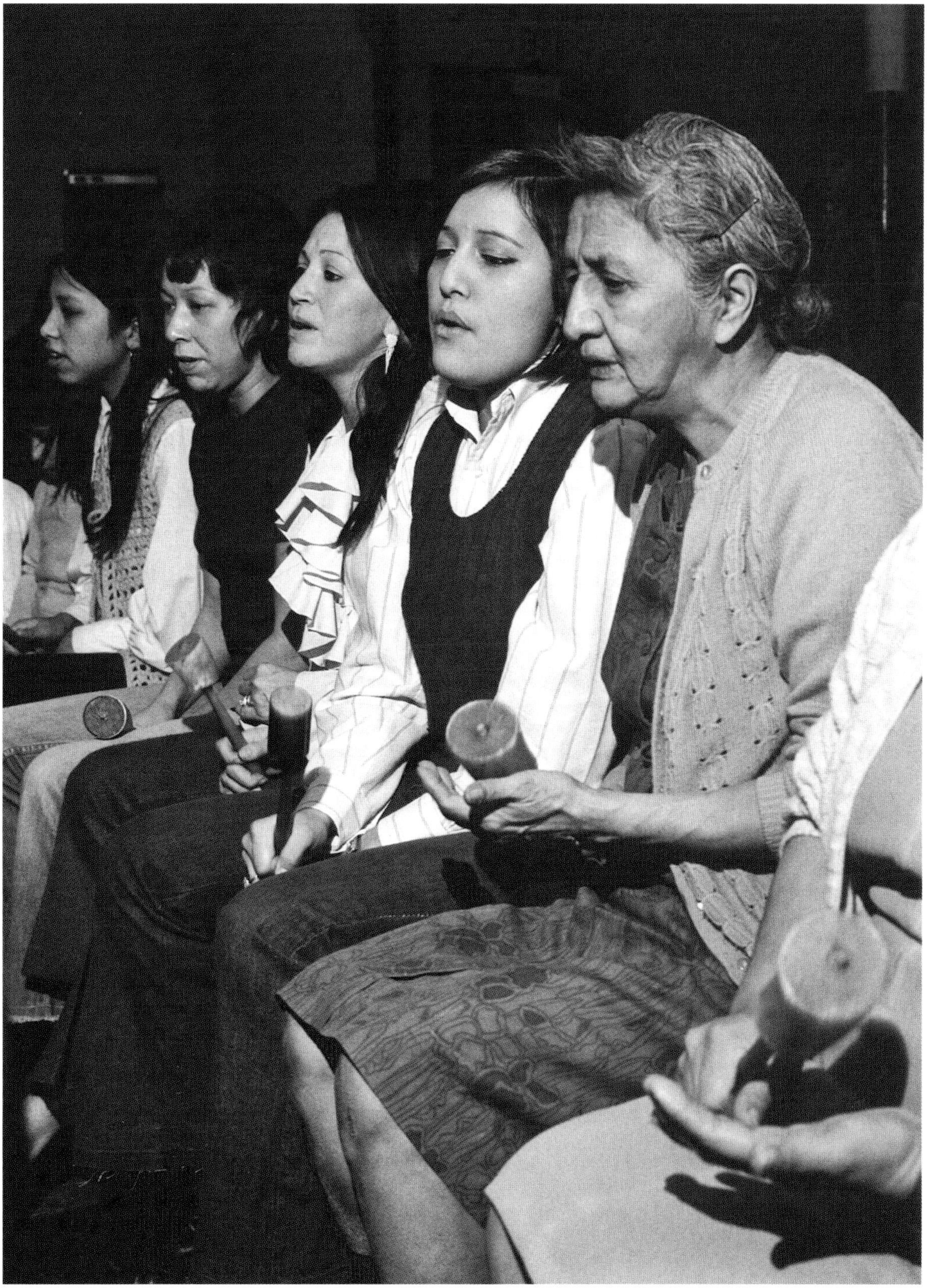

and this continuance comes
in lacrosse jackets and
work shirts and formal
dresses and blouses
and T-shirts and jeans,
and earrings and pompadours
brilliant with Brylcream
as well as ribbon shirts and
beaded velvet collars and
garments cut from treaty cloth and

we know the clothes
don't make the man
and don't make the woman.

It is instead the place
in memory that awakens
when the benches appear
in the room's center and
rattles and drums materialize
in hands already intimate
with the shapes of their handles
and sticks and carved rounded bellies

and here we are, like them
awake and aware, the songs
of these silent photographs
filling our ears like a pulse
when we are straining
to keep ourselves going
singing and dancing

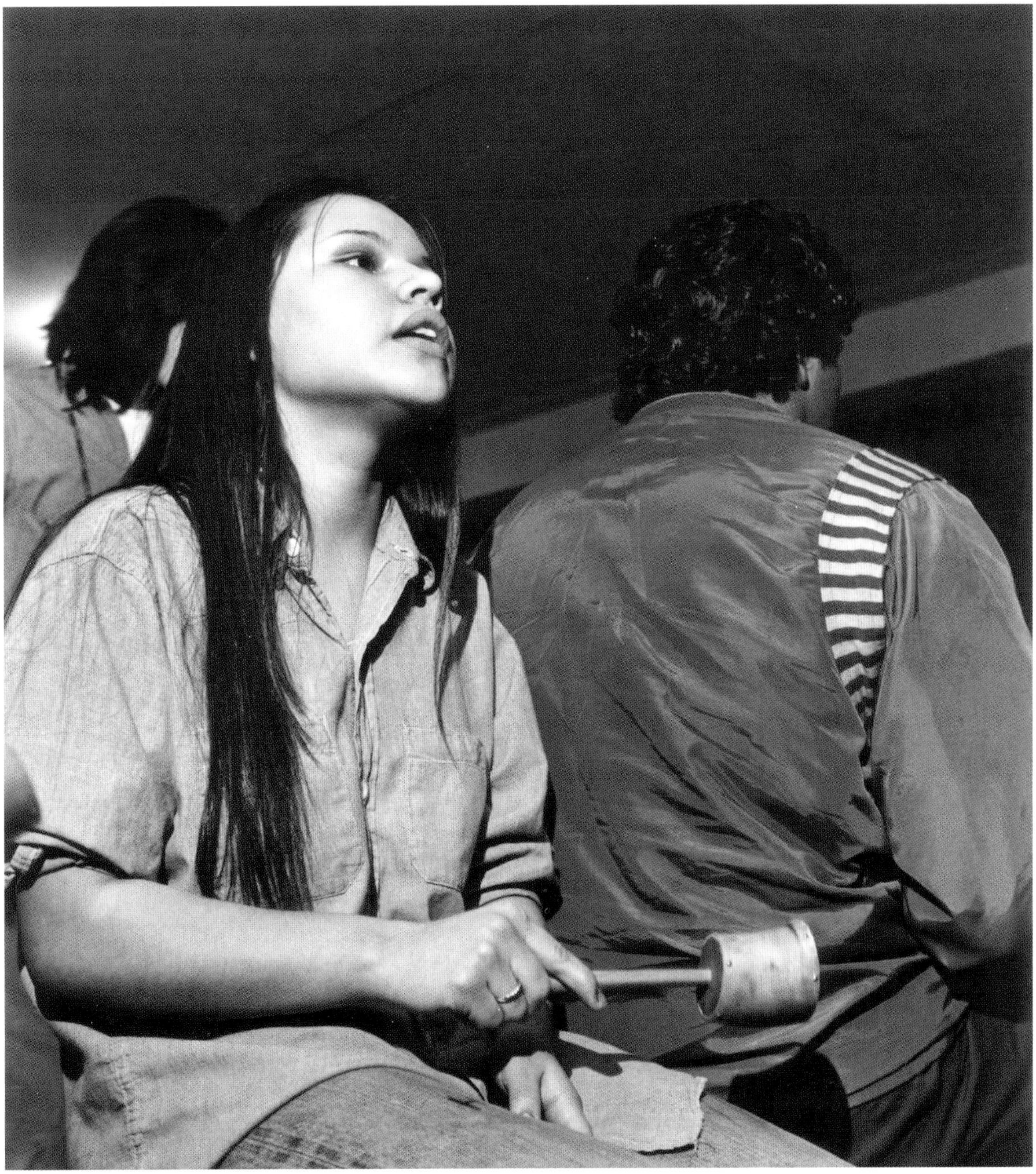

when we are not sure
we have one more dance
or one more song left
in these legs and lungs
but their dedication
gives us our dedication
because if they could do it
we can do it, and yes,
it's a Friday night
and yes, it's been a long week

but when you get in that room
with so much history and family
there will be nothing left to do
but smile and laugh and mingle breath
and taste the frybread, dunk it
in cornsoup and wash it down
with strawberry drink

and know that body and blood
is not solely the ritual
of one group

that we each share blood
and body on this floor
and that is how
an adjective becomes a noun
how Social is a way of being
and not a description
of the ways we should behave.

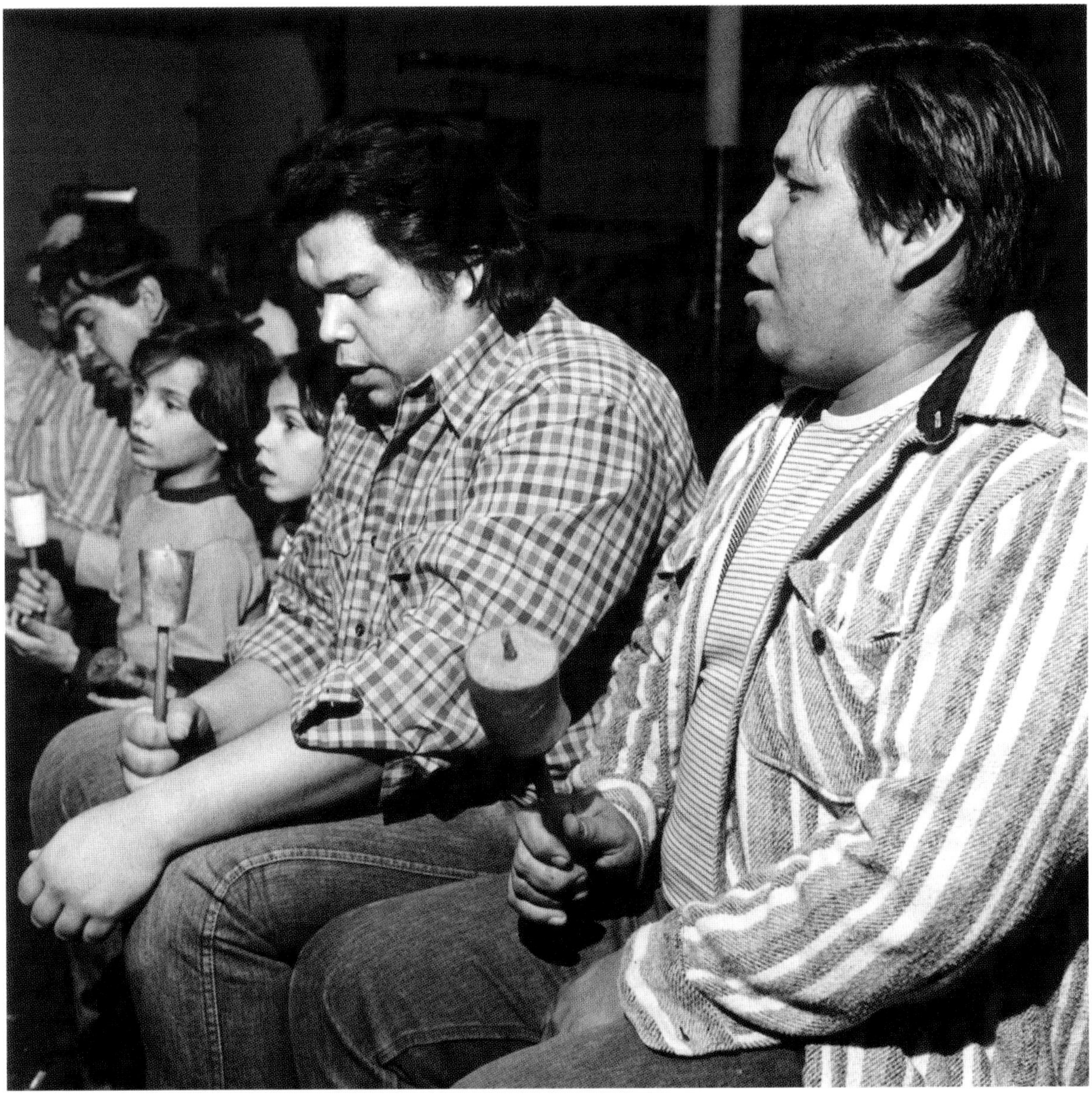

Whether we sit or stand,
pressing ourselves together
in this small room
you know we will still be
around long after photos
of us have lost our names
and the details of our time.

Essence will vibrate
from your hand to mine
and from mine to another
and in that way, accounting
for variation in human
talents, we carry on.

No matter where the room
is located, we will find ourselves
and our own way
home.

Tiny Chief

From an aerosol can,
spraying a buzz
and dark particles
of stain, in the arcs
of young hands, mixing
upper and lower case
letters indiscriminately

a message is left behind
for years traced haphazardly
in paint and brick and mortar
framing them, the way
they have perhaps been
cast in different portraits
through their lives.

The vestibule, engraved
above their heads
carefully and rigidly
in a font meant to evoke
a utilitarian and functional
public education suggests
they have received
the means to move forward
in this other place

where they wear white
to say they know the world
they will wrestle with
where darkness in clothes
or skin is always a metaphor
with negative connotations.

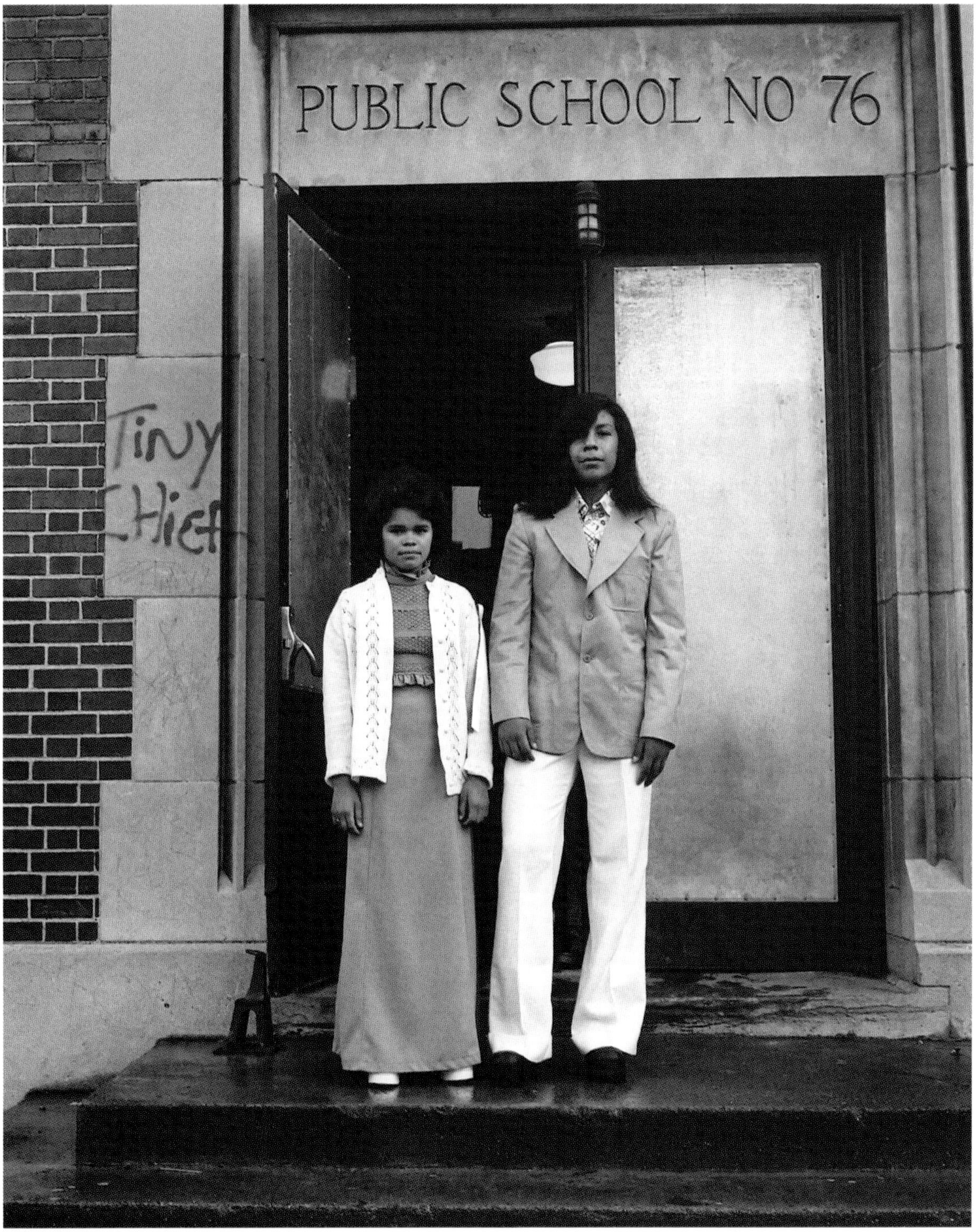
PUBLIC SCHOOL NO 76
Tiny
Chief

Years go by rapidly
once grades and classrooms
and three months of freedom
give way to jobs and joblessness
where those white pants and sweater
go the way of such formalities.

It won't be long
before her dark arms
reveal, from beneath
those delicate knit
sweater arms,
a primitive tattoo—
ink from a ball-point pen
staining the layers of skin
pierced with a sewing needle,
a man's name scarred
on her wrist forever,
longer than the man
himself sticks around,
a reminder of the injuries
we incur and accept
with such matter of fact indifference
that we forget they are there.

"Bob?" she might respond
when asked, "some guy I knew
when I was a different person"
and here she is, that newer
different person, leaning
in a different doorway, the sharpness

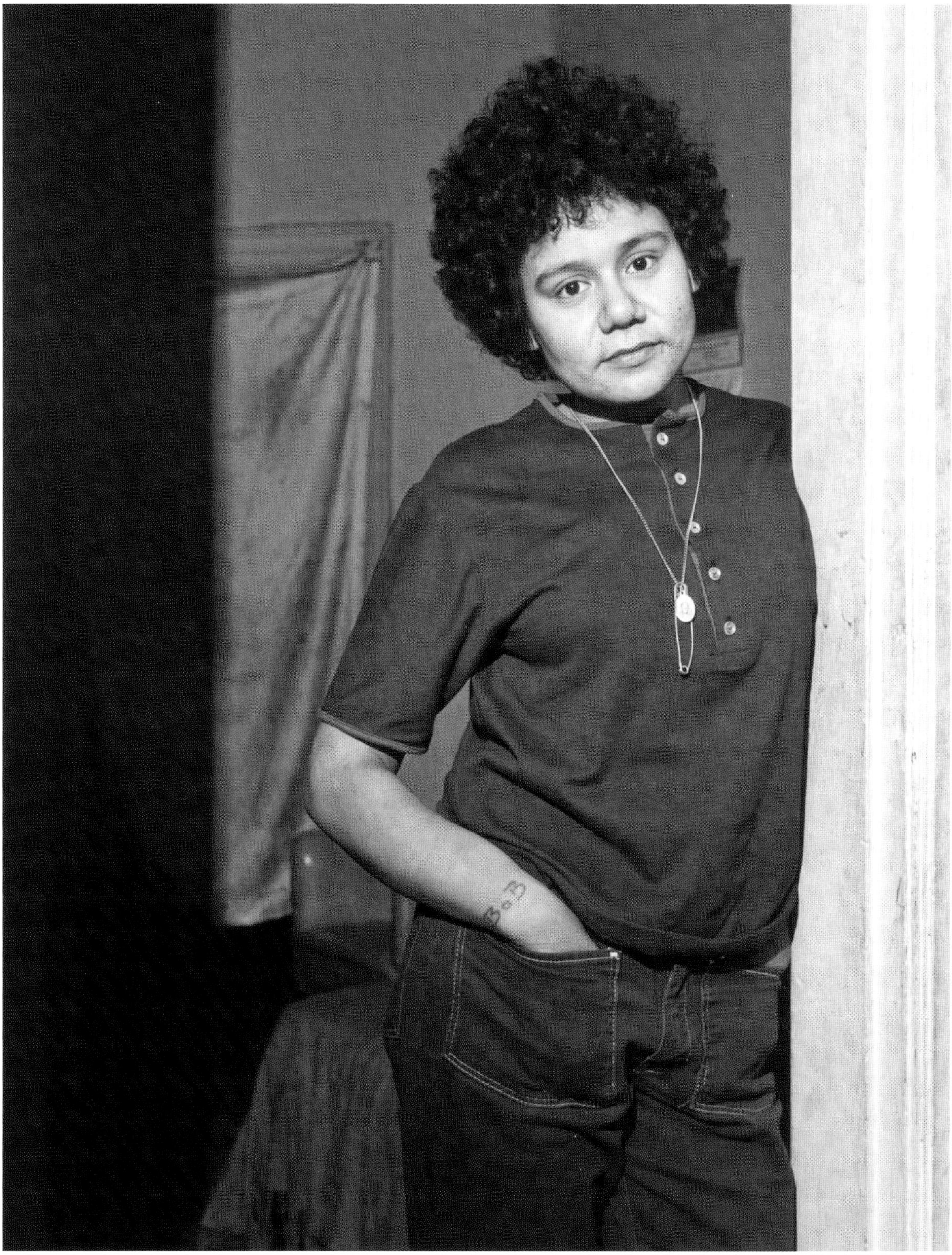

of needle under skin as distant a memory
as that day she left
the entrance of PUBLIC SCHOOL NO. 76
for the last time.

And stripped of dress jacket
and white bell bottoms,
he holds his hands
folded in front of him,
maybe in defense
no trace on his face
of the hopeful smile
that had accompanied him
in the school door,
owning for the fleeting moment
that label of Tiny Chief
perhaps believing all he needed
were formal clothes, a diploma
and faith to make his own way
in the world, convinced
he had the necessary equipment

but it is not long after
as he stands with another
young woman, leaning on him
as if he were immobile
before a chain-link fence
and a sidewalk being slowly removed—
even concrete no match

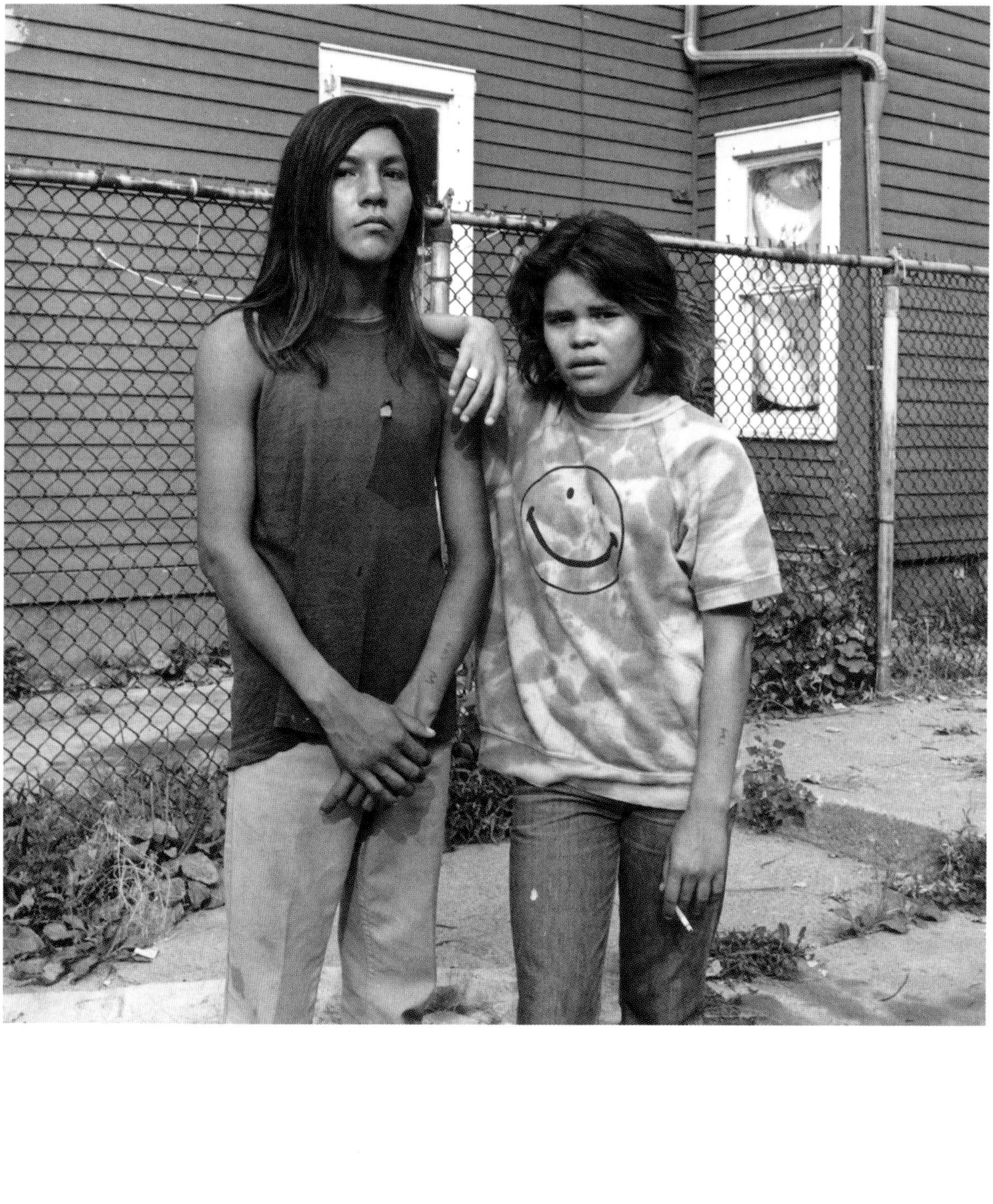

for the relentless
survival tactics hardwired
into the DNA of weeds.

They look into the camera,
the only happy face the one
silk-screened on her shirt,
in her fingers a cigarette
to deflect any impression
she might be young
and impressionable.

With that look,
and the hole on her jeans
and the same sized hole
across the chest
of his shirt,
just above the heart,
she could banish
her past self,
before the cigarette
in her left hand
and the ring glinting
on her right,
where she nearly smiles
riding a bicycle
a peace sign sewn on
to the knee of her jeans
a symbol of optimism
and desire or just a patch
covering a spot

where the fabric has given
way in a place
where the budget requires
them to hold on
a little while longer,
banish her old world
where she bought the idea
that a patch could work
and that no-one would know
the difference, the kind of story
a mother can tell her child
for only so many years
before neither can bear its lie.

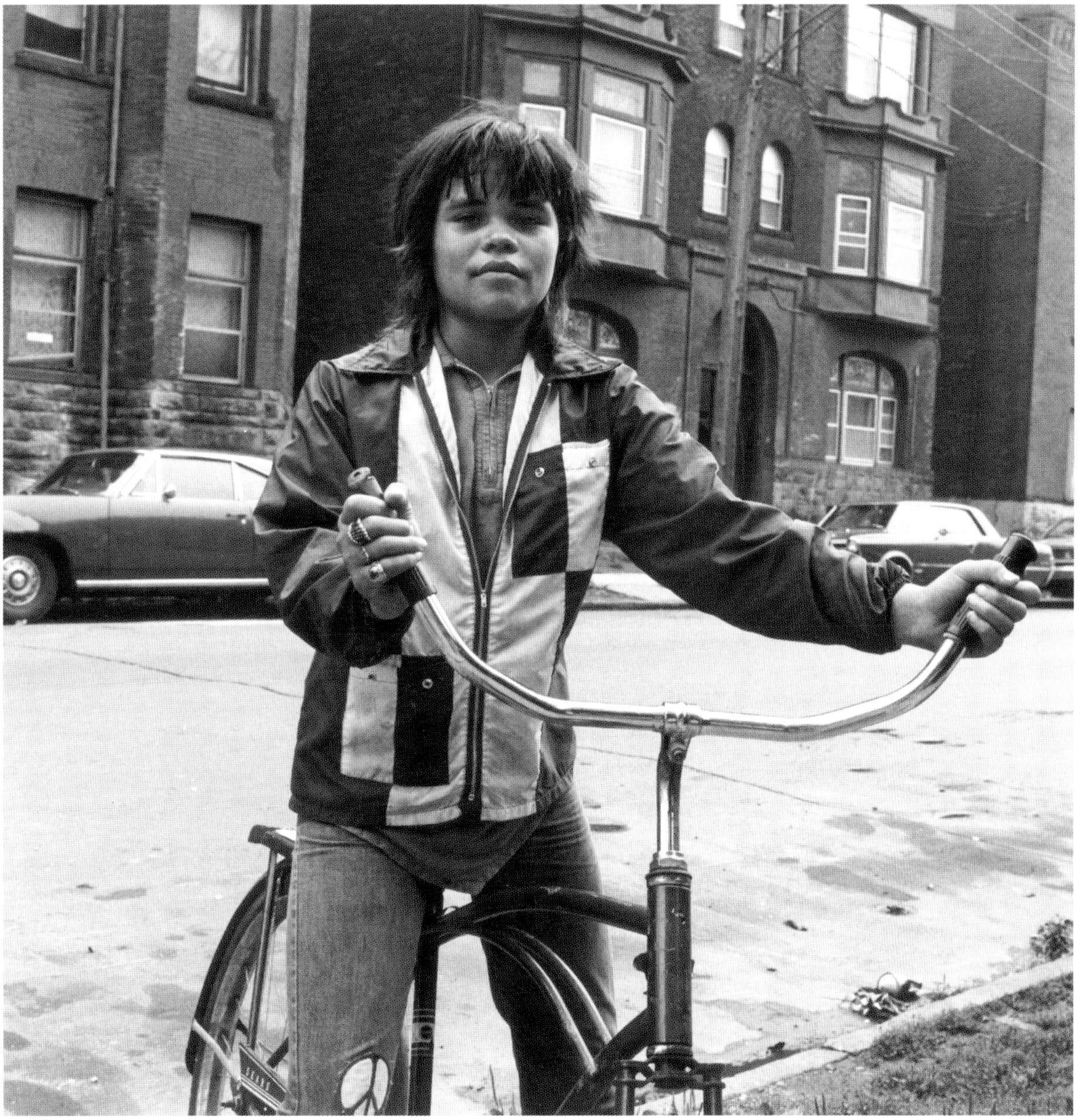

Door to Door

Wood, weathered, and graying
splits under the weight
of the ways
we come and go from within
this door to home.

This door—wood and glass,
nails rusting at the seams
where grain meets grain,
where one beam joins the next—
rests uneasy on its hinges,
bending with the weight
of gravity and years,
like our own spines
as we move forward,
hoping to find frames
that will keep us
standing straight
holding on
for maybe one more winter
ignoring the snow
that drifts and gathers
in the entry
amid muddy and salty boots
and stiff rawhide gloves
like white velvet
waiting for a dreamer
to pick up a needle
and bead us some dreams.

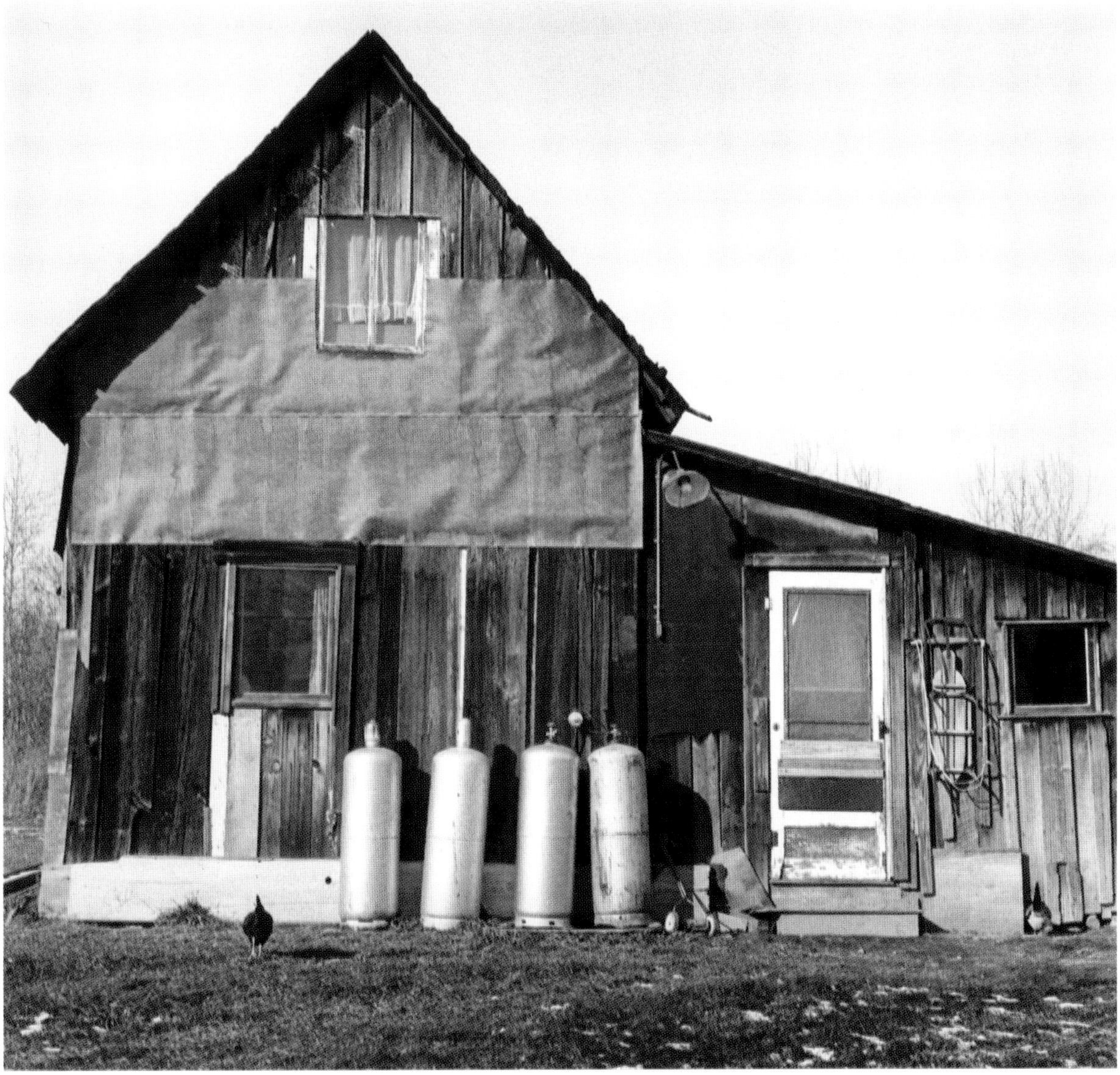

Splinters from these beams
sometimes catch
our toughened skin
working their way
beneath to those highways
carrying our blood
to and from our hearts
like those asphalt roads
and dirt lanes
we know so well.

Shadows and sun hit the house
in equal measure as we fan
while the temperature sinks
and the earth hardens
beneath our feet
going dead for a few months
and we are confident
that when spring comes
and the sun stays
longer, casting deeper
corners of darkness,
the ground will free itself,
the way our joints do
after coffee and movement
in later mornings.

So for now we stand there,
some times even bare footed, risking
the way those shards break the seals
of our calloused soles, keeping a barrier

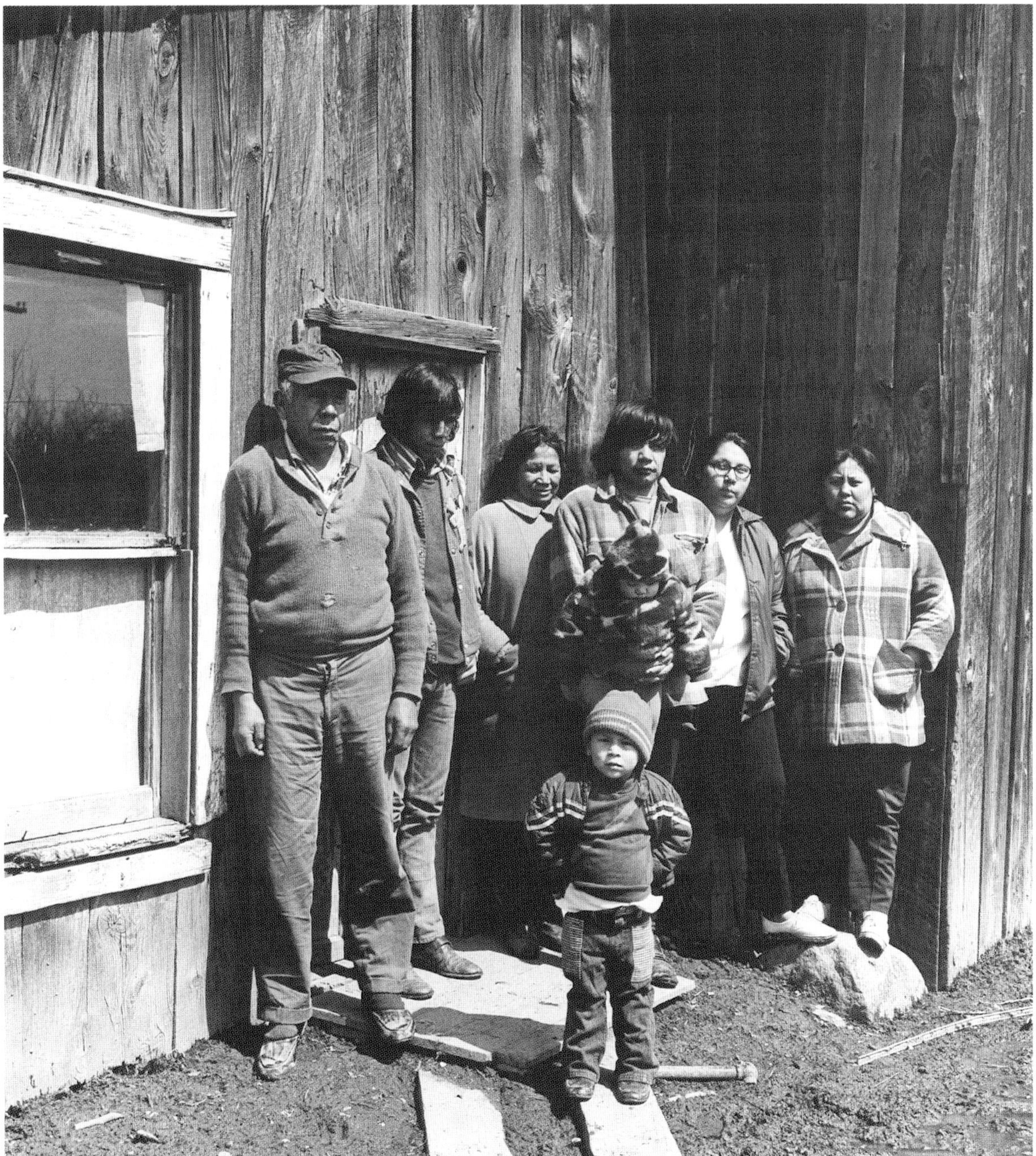

from the mud we will join
soon enough.

And against this ill-fitting door
and the mortar chipping,
flaking from outer walls,
keeping the wind from us
where wind and wood reveal
grain and all the ways
nature ignores human attempts
to shape it, make it more orderly,
we track days by night, counting
the shape and movement
of our evolving grandmother
moon sliding across the sky
surrounded by those brothers
as they dance their way
through the cycles
that help us to remember
the different ways
we say thank you.

Like the dogs who rule
reservation roads reminding us
always that territory is real
with the ways they patrol, even
when the temperature drops
so low those pads bleed
red tracks all the way home,
and yet, stand with us
balancing on hind legs

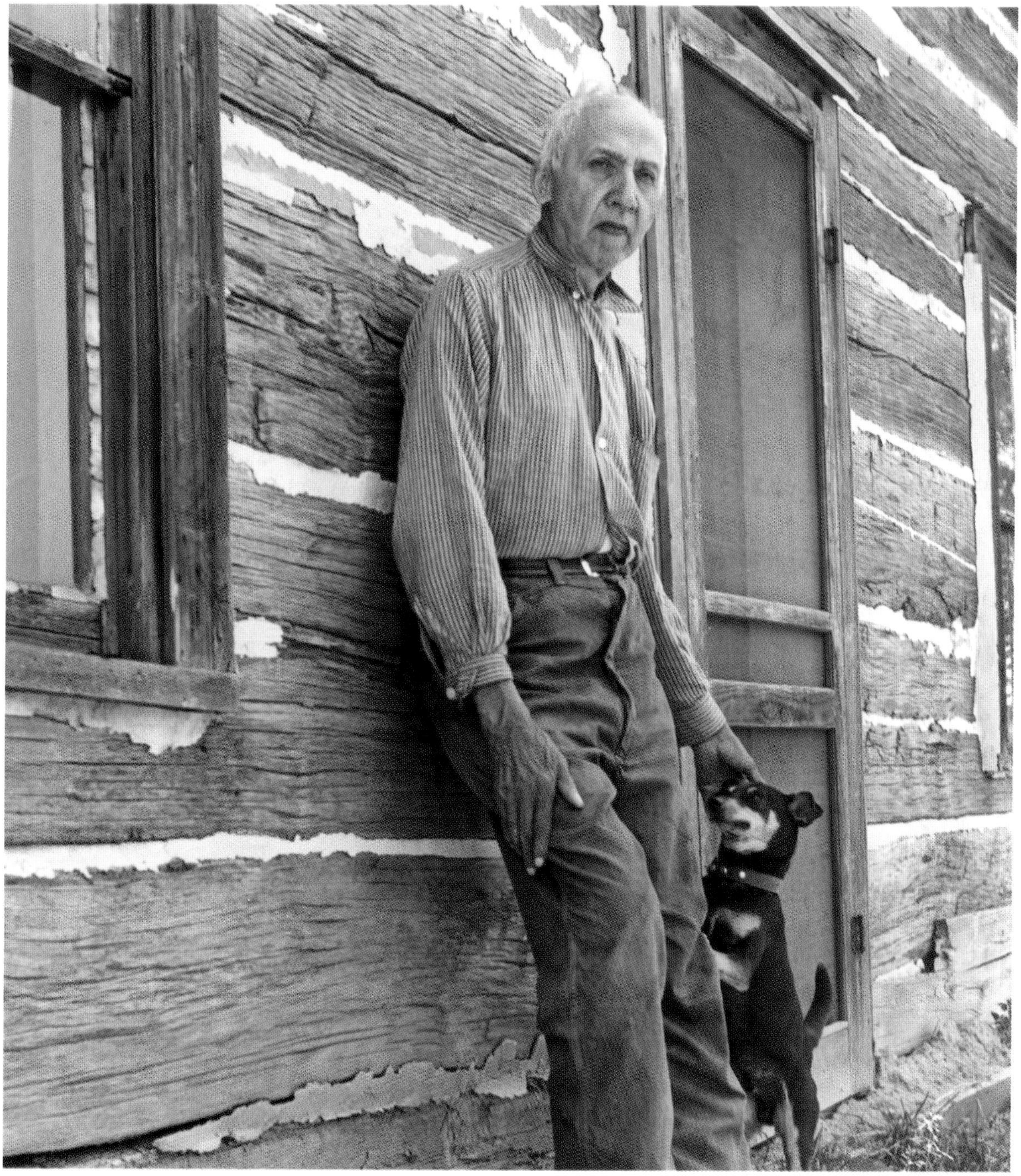

defying gravity and anatomy,
we learn to celebrate loyalty
but maybe not as well as a creature
whose lifespan is compressed
seven years to one
can understand.

But despite our best
intentions to stay, redefine
family in variation
and familiarity, sometimes
we leave that Western Door
behind and discover new worlds
beyond the protection of
relatives or history or treaties
or all of the above

and sometimes we find ourselves
alone in city clothes,
work-roughed skin replaced
with shiny black leather jackets,
chrome zippers closing in
on wrists that had grown to fullness
wrapped in wool mittens
around hand-me-down flannel shirts,
and we think we are
tough and new,
disregarding the winters
from home and the ways we learned
to layer, keeping warm
on those frozen roads

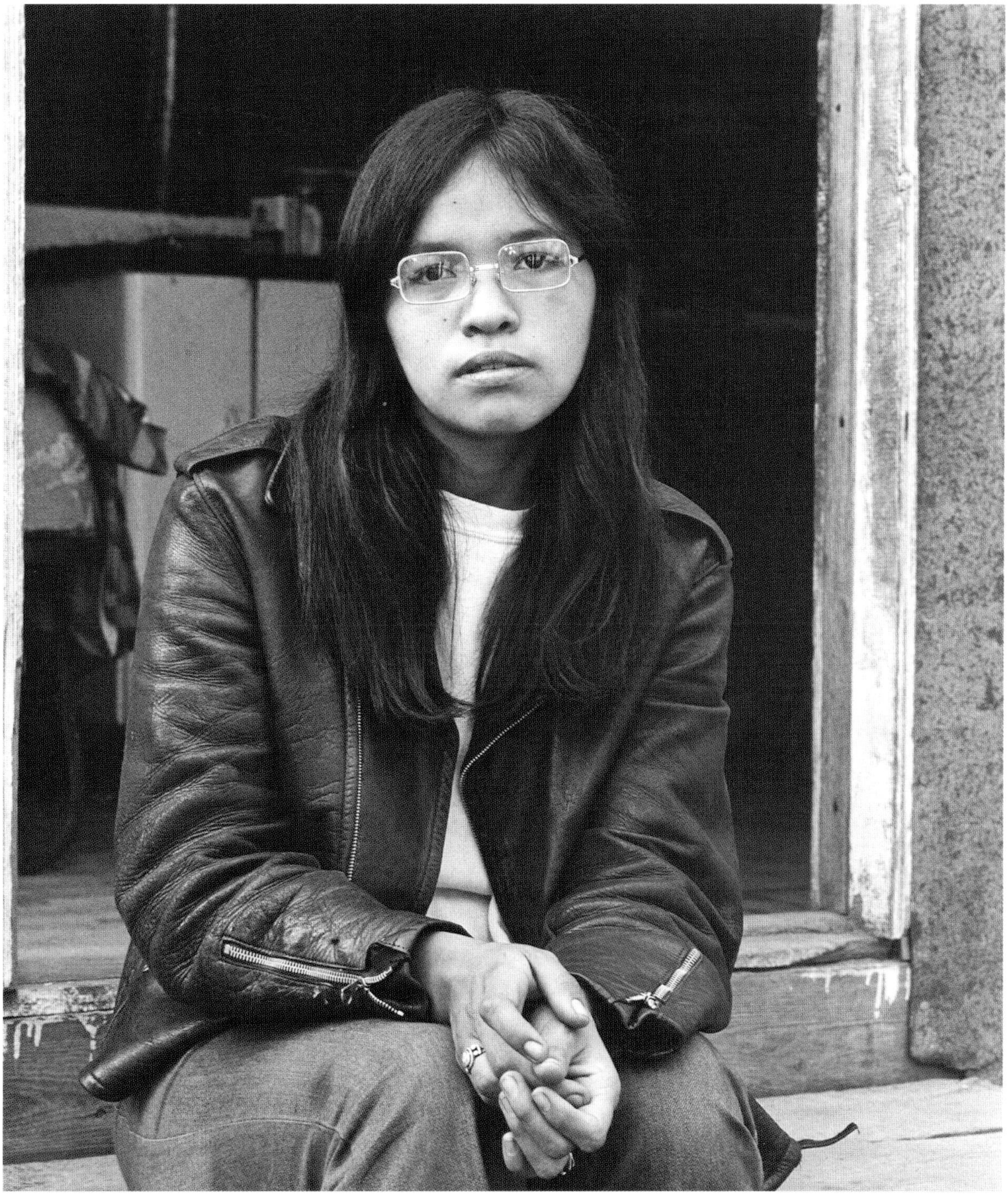

with long stretches of woods
where houses only appeared
distant on the horizon,
and we cut our hair, thinking
that would make us indistinguishable
from everyone else, but as always
we find ourselves doors to be near
just the trace and echo of home
framing that formidable leather and metal.

These new steps
we fall in love with.
Concrete, firm, unwavering and
splinter-free, they suggest
all the things we have left
were deserving of abandonment

but the stone in cast concrete
is not as enduring
as we had believed
and though we will discover
that falling on concrete
comes with a different price
than falling on dirt
and even wood is more forgiving,

we will notice at some point
that concrete chips and flakes
away like anything else

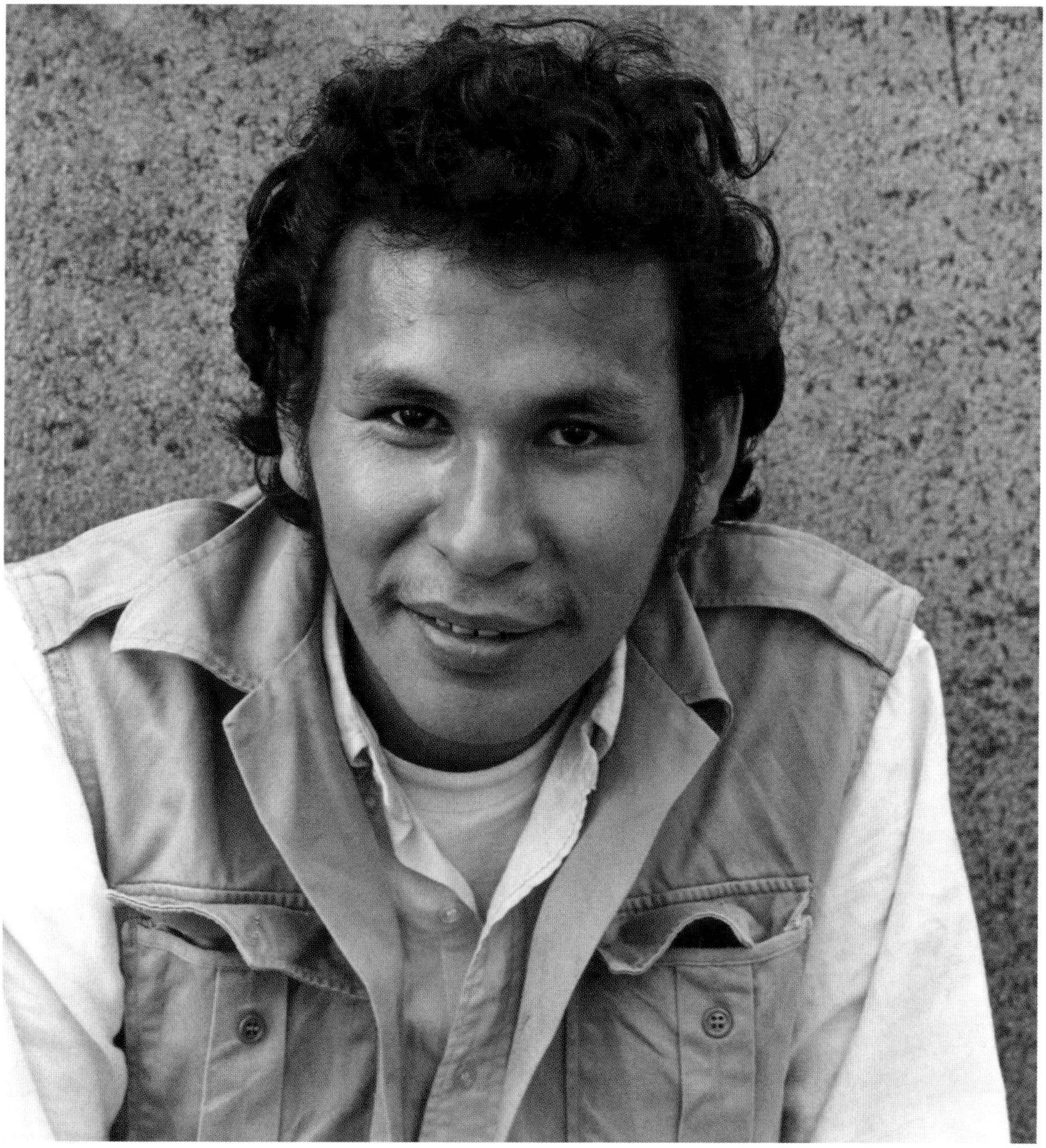

and then maybe we will find
the answer we thought
we were looking for.

It won't be from the steps
leading up to these new places
where distance between homes
is measured in feet instead of miles

but in the warmth of the person
sitting close, knees touching
only slightly, enough to feel
the heat of another body
the beat of another heart.

We should have known
better anyway and we would
have, if we'd only observed
the ways we respond,
when a stranger arrives,

and maybe we will see
when he comes back
and hands us the photos
he has taken, that
when that man with the camera
appeared on these anonymous
Lower West Side streets,

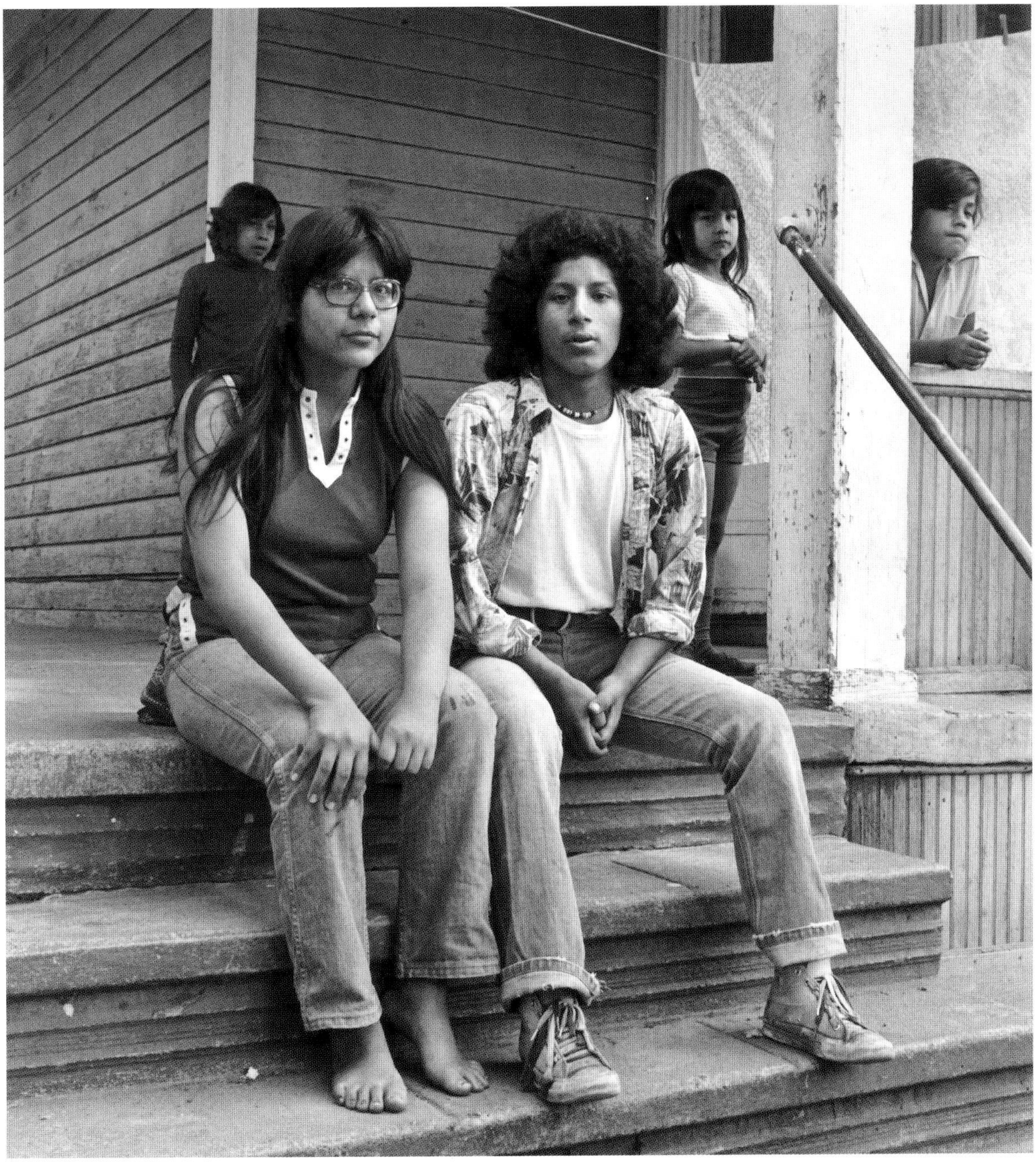

we reasserted our DNA, our blood,
smiled our familiarity,
flung arms around shoulders
where the pulse in a wrist
beats out that consistent rhythm
against the shoulder of another,
the ways we touch one another
not inadvertent and unintentional
but assured and confident,
even through those tough
city clothes and transient
identities we might try on
in those new places,
and we reacquainted ourselves
with each other,
Skin to skin.

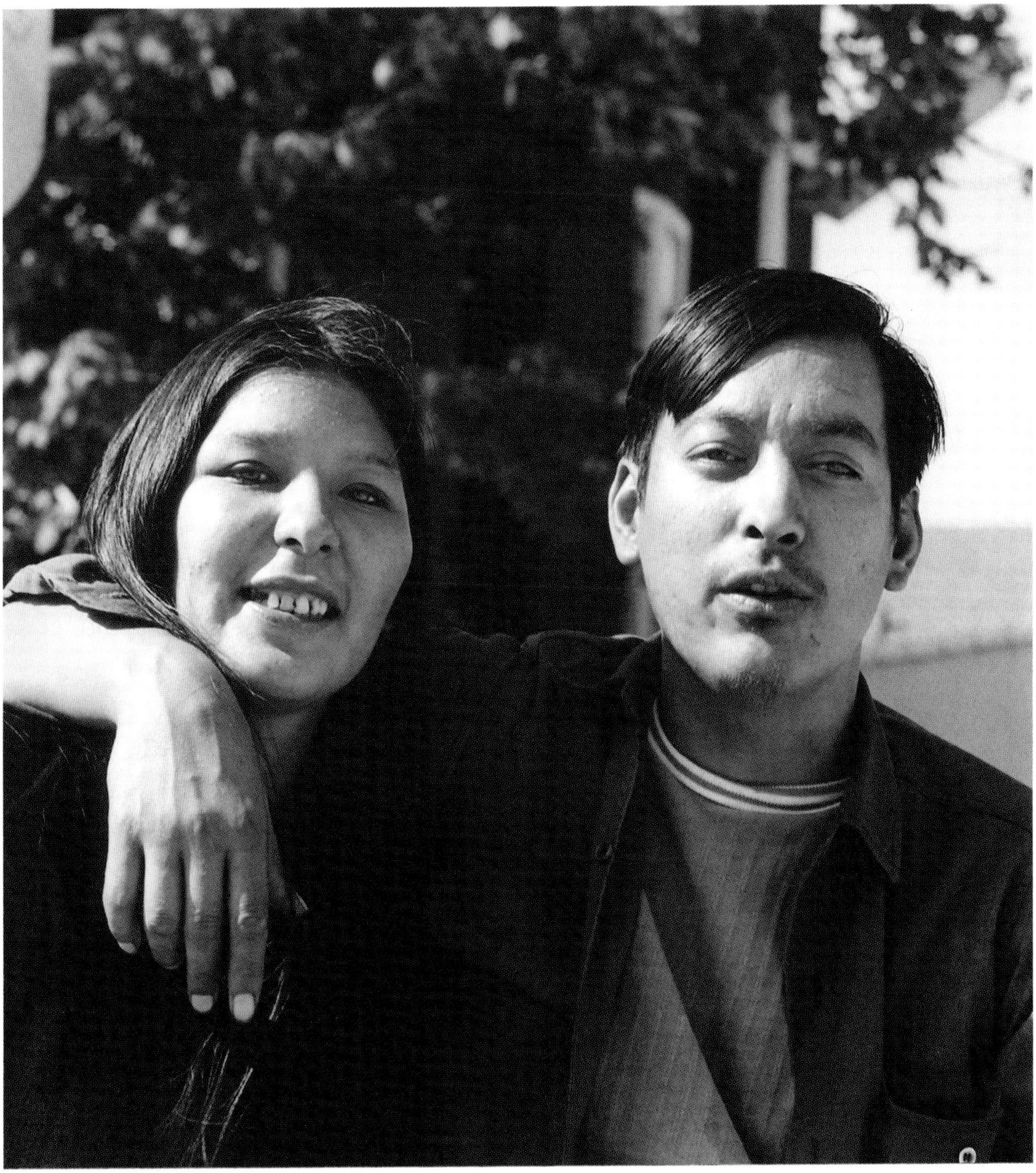

Milton Rogovin

A practicing optometrist until an assault by the House Un-American Activities Committee, Milton Rogovin began his second career as a social documentary photographer in 1957. His subjects spanned the Storefront Churches of Buffalo, Pablo Neruda's Chile, the Family of Miners, Working People, the Yemeni and Native American community and the Lower West Side, a neighborhood where Milton Rogovin photographed families for thirty years.

Rogovin's photographic archive is at the Library of Congress in Washington, D.C., and the Center for Creative Photography at the University of Arizona in Tucson. Publications, films and traveling exhibitions bring his photography around the globe. His extensive website features photographic portfolios for classroom use.

Throughout his fifty-year photograhic career, Milton Rogovin, along with his wife Anne, chronicled the lives of poor and working people in eleven nations. He stated of his journey, "The rich have their own photographers, I choose to photograph the forgotten ones." Milton is ninety-nine years old and living in Buffalo, surrounded by his photography and family.

Photograph by Mark Rogovin

Eric Gansworth

Eric Gansworth (Onondaga) is Lowery Writer-in-Residence and Professor of English at Canisius College in Buffalo, New York. He was born and raised at the Tuscarora Nation. The author of seven books, including the PEN Oakland Award winning *Mending Skins*, and *A Half-Life of Cardio-Pulmonary Function* (National Book Critics Circle's "Good Reads List" for Sprimg 2008), Gansworth is also a visual artist, and generally incorporates paintings as integral elements into his narratives. In the fall of 2008, his first full-length dramatic work, *Re-Creation Story,* was part of the Public Theater's Native Theater Festival in New York City. His work has been widely shown and anthologized and has appeared in *The Kenyon Review, The New York Quarterly, Stone Canoe, Shenandoah, The Boston Review, Third Coast,* and *The Yellow Medicine Review,* among others. His next book, *Extra Indians,* a novel, will be published by Milkweed Editions in 2010.

Photograph by Shaun M. Maciejewski

Donors

As this book goes to press, the Rogovin family prepares to celebrate Milton's 100th birthday. With thanks to the following, who helped make this book possible:

Barbara Armentrout
Rhoda and Hank Berstein
Denah S. Bookstein
Ezra Bookstein
Priscilla Bowen
Lisa R. Brand
Lois Bridges
Regina Chiou Browett
David Budbill
Janice and Ed Dabney
Frank & Louise Farkas
Ilene and Jim Gilbert
Margaret F. Guthrie
Robert Hirsch
Maxine Insera
Kate Koperski
June E. Licence
Brian Lindquist
Paul Lossowski
Walt & Nancy Nygard
Stephanie Pincus
Linda Shed Priebe
Dr. Jennifer Ruh
Pete and Toshi Seeger
Gary Stenger
Judie Takacs
Jerri Zbiral & Alan Teller
Georgia Wever
Nancy Willick